Race Unequals

Race Unequals

Overseer Contracts, White Masculinities, and the Formation of Managerial Identity in the Plantation Economy

Teri A. McMurtry-Chubb

LEXINGTON BOOKS
Lanham • Boulder • New York • London

Published by Lexington Books
An imprint of The Rowman & Littlefield Publishing Group, Inc.
4501 Forbes Boulevard, Suite 200, Lanham, Maryland 20706
www.rowman.com

Copyright © 2021 The Rowman & Littlefield Publishing Group, Inc.

All rights reserved. No part of this book may be reproduced in any form or by any electronic or mechanical means, including information storage and retrieval systems, without written permission from the publisher, except by a reviewer who may quote passages in a review.

British Library Cataloguing in Publication Information Available

Library of Congress Cataloging-in-Publication Data

Names: McMurtry-Chubb, Teri A., author.
Title: Race unequals : overseer contracts, white masculinities, and the formation of managerial identity in the plantation economy / Teri A. McMurtry-Chubb.
Description: Lanham : Lexington Books, [2021] | Includes bibliographical references and index. | Summary: "Race Unequals: Overseer Contracts, White Masculinities, and the Formation of Managerial Identity in the Plantation Economy is a re-imagining of the plantation not as Black and White, but in shades of White male identity. Through an examination of employment contracts between plantation owners and their overseers, and the web of public and private law that surrounded them, this book challenges notions of a monolithic White male identity in the antebellum South. It considers how race provided White men access to the land and enslaved labor that were foundational to the plantation economy, but how the wealthiest of those men used contracts, public law, and plantation management schemes to limit the access points by which overseers, the first managerial class in the United States, could achieve upward mobility as both White people and as men. In navigating the legal and social parameters of their employment contracts, overseers negotiated a white masculinity that formed their managerial identity. This managerial identity carried the imprint of white supremacy necessary to preserve inequities on the plantation, and perhaps in our modern workplaces as well"— Provided by publisher.
Identifiers: LCCN 2021004183 (print) | LCCN 2021004184 (ebook) | ISBN 9781498599061 (cloth) | ISBN 9781498599085 (pbk) | ISBN 9781498599078 (epub)
Subjects: LCSH: Plantations—Economic aspects—Southern States—History—19th century. | Plantation overseers—Southern States—History—19th century. | Plantations—Southern States—Management—History—19th century. | Whites—Race identity—Southern States—History—19th century. | Masculinity—Southern States—History—19th century.
Classification: LCC HD1471.U52 S6863 2021 (print) | LCC HD1471.U52 (ebook) | DDC 331.11/734097509034—dc23
LC record available at https://lccn.loc.gov/2021004183
LC ebook record available at https://lccn.loc.gov/2021004184

Contents

Acknowledgments		vii
Introduction: The World the Planters Made		xi
1	The Overseer, His Contracts, and His Contractual Relationships	1
2	Profitable Planters, Industrious Overseers, Maintaining the Status Quo	15
3	"Pushing" Torture, Managing Violence, and Planter Regulation of Overseer Control	31
4	White Masculinities, Private Law, and the Battle for Social Control	65
5	Immoral Men, Immoral Ends, Deference as Social Death	83
Epilogue: The "Lost Cause" and the Legacy of Plantation Management		97
Bibliography		107
Index		117
About the Author		125

Acknowledgments

First, I thank God, without whom not one word of this book would exist. Your blessings throughout this project have been continuous, unfolding, and astounding. Thank you for holding this space for me to walk in and out of, and finally into again. Together we finally got this one done. I thank my husband, Mark Anthony Chubb, for his love and unshakable belief in me. I also thank him for his patience as we lugged boxes of archival records back and forth across the country as our callings called and our occupations required. Mark, you have an extraordinary ability, a prescient understanding of when purpose meets opportunity. Thank you for your persistence and support in making sure I too see and understand. I also thank your family, my father-in-law Eddie C. Chubb Sr., and the legacy of the free Black town, Chubbtown, for helping me to grasp southern agriculture and rural life. Before his input, the rhythm of farming and the back-breaking work of planting and chopping cotton were things I had read about, but hadn't touched or fully understood.

There are librarians and scholars who aided my research and grounded my thinking on the antebellum south. I am indebted to the librarians at the University of Iowa University Archives and Special Collections. Over my two years of almost daily archival research, you were kind, courteous, and beyond helpful. To Raizel Liebler at UIC John Marshall Law School, you are proof that librarians, especially law librarians, are indeed superheroes and do wear capes. Thank you for your heavy lifting to get me all of the resources and access I needed even during a worldwide pandemic.

A project of this scope and interdisciplinarity would not have been at all possible without the depth and intelligence of my professors and mentors. First on that list are my parents. Thank you Harold A. McMurtry Sr. and Dorothy L. McMurtry for instilling in me a work ethic and curiosity about the world that supported your vision for me that I could be anything and do anything as long as I could imagine it. I was and am crazy enough to believe you both. Thanks to Dr. Dalila DeSousa, Dr. Tiffany Patterson, and Dean Cynthia Neal Spence in the history, sociology, and anthropology departments at Spelman College, my alma mater, for teaching me the foundations of Black feminist thought, and for how to view history, gender, and the law through an African Diasporic gaze. Thank you Dr. Michael Gomez, Dr. Lidwien Kapteijns, and Dr. Jonathan Knudsen for helping me to understand empire. Special thanks to the Graduate College and Department of History at the University of Iowa, especially Dr. Leslie Schwalm, Dr. Shel Stromquist, and Dr. Linda K. Kerber, for helping me to see the American South, gender, and labor through your lenses, pushing our cohort ever left in our thinking, and teaching us how to make history present in our classrooms and in our organizing.

I am grateful for the behind-the-scenes work of many, including the work of the sweetest, kindest, most skillful research assistant, Diantha Ellis. Thank you for organizing the hundreds of pages of archival documents into a neat database. Thanks for taking us digital. Without your work, I would have been lost and so too would the stories in this book. Thank you for reading early chapters of this book, along with Haley McCoy, and to both of you for cheering me on. Resounding thanks to my attorney and friend, Sha-Shana Crichton, for providing her time and expertise in helping to bring this book to print.

Finally, I dedicate to this book to the enslaved men and women whose lives are in every crevice of its pages. My gratefulness extends particularly to the enslaved men and women on the Joseph M. Jaynes Plantation: Lousan, Minden, Cely, Nancy, Tempe, Eliza, Martha, Violet, Pharaby, Caroline, Little Eliza, Esther, Harriet, Sarah Ann, [Young] Cely, Ella, Missouri Ann, Louisa, Julia Ann, Nelly, Virginia, Edmund, Big George, Amon, John, Fedric, Jim, Little George, Hampton, Jesse, Daniel, Adam, Edward, Albert, Pinkey, Enyalds, Scott, Calvin, Breckenridge, Huston, and Thomas Ervin. For the past fifteen years you have helped me to teach about the brutality and cold efficiency of the plantation economy. You have also guided me as I have taught in classrooms, given lectures, and lived as an example of your strength, the strength of our people, and what you made possible because of your many sacrifices. I extend that thanks to all of the enslaved individuals in this study unnamed and those in the court and archival records whose names appear throughout this book. You will never be forgotten. You are never far from my thoughts.

I too dedicate this book to the overseers in the archival records, who, like their charge to drive African bodies endlessly and to the point of death in pursuit of money and power, also drove this study. I write your names here to remember you also: Vincent A. Peirson, E. B. Whiddon, William A. Collins, David T. Weeks, Robert W. Miller, J. M. Key, William F. Black, Parker

Carradine, Asa Kemp, Charles B. Crocker, and Thomas E. Senoir. Whether you understood that your work contributed to systems of oppression that imperil us all, or whether you saw the plantation as a path forward to monetary wealth and improved social status, we might not yet know. Whatever your reasons, your journey provides relevant context for our current world. May what you teach us in these pages show your descendants that their fate is bound up in the bodies of the formerly enslaved Africans and their descendants. If your descendants work to get themselves free, then maybe we can all be truly free together.

Introduction
The World the Planters Made

In book *Twelve Years A Slave* by Solomon Northup, Northup describes a series of exchanges with five White men that almost lead to his slow and painful death by hanging: William Ford, his enslaver and owner of Bayou Boeuf Plantation in Louisiana;[1] Mr. Chapin, Ford's overseer at the Bayou Boeuf Plantation in Louisiana;[2] John M. Tibeats, a yeoman farmer/carpenter to whom Northup is later sold by a chattel mortgage of four hundred dollars (held by Ford);[3] and Cook and Ramsay, two of Tibeats' friends, overseers from neighboring plantations.[4] Of Tibeats, Northup remarked that he was

> the opposite of Ford in all respects. He was a small, crabbed, quick tempered, spiteful man. He had no fixed residence that I ever heard of, but passed from one plantation to another wherever he could find employment. He was without standing in the community, not esteemed by white men or even respected by slaves. He was ignorant, withal, and of a revengeful disposition.[5]

Northup recounts an interaction between himself and Tibeats where both were building a weaving house at Bayou Boeuf.[6] Tibeats instructed Northup to get nails for the project from Mr. Chapin.[7] Northup complied, but Tibeats later found fault with the type of nails used and attempted to physically attack Northup with Chapin's three feet long braided rawhide whip.[8] Northup retaliated and whipped Tibeats instead, an act punishable by death.[9] Tibeats's response was to ride to get Cook and Ramsay, and all three attempted to hang Northup from a tree.[10] Mr. Chapin, a pistol in each hand, intervened. Northup recalled Chapin's words:

> Gentlemen, I have a few words to say. You had better listen to them. Whoever moves that slave another foot from where he stands is a dead man. In the first

place, he does not deserve this treatment. It is a shame to murder him in this manner. I never knew a more faithful boy than [Northup]. You, Tibeats, are in the fault yourself. You are pretty much of a scoundrel, and I know it, and you richly deserve the flogging you have received. *In the next place, I have been the overseer on this plantation for seven years, and, in the absence of William Ford, am master here. My duty is to protect his interests, and that duty I shall perform.* You are not responsible-you are a worthless fellow. Ford holds a mortgage on [Northup] of four hundred dollars. If you hang him, he loses his debt. Until that is canceled you have no right to take his life. You have no right to take it any way. There is a law for a slave as well as for the white man. You are no better than a murderer.[11]

Chapin then ordered Tibeats to leave and ordered the overseers back to their respective plantations. However, he did not attempt to move Northup or cut him down from the tree.[12] The reader considers the chilling scene: Northup is hanging from the tree, Chapin is pacing the porch of his home after dispatching an enslaved person to get the master, and Tibeats is plotting Northup's death even as he leaves the plantation.[13] Northup hangs from the tree all day until Ford arrives at sunset and cuts him down.[14] Ford subsequently entrusts Chapin with Northup's protection from Tibeats through the night.[15] As manager, the overseer must protect the master's property above all else.

This scene was later dramatized in the movie version of *Twelve Years A Slave*. As this encounter between enslaved, yeoman, overseer, and master is brought to life in vivid color, the viewer sees Mr. Northup hanging from a noose, Spanish moss clouding his vision, and balancing on his toes so not to break his neck while the plantation mistress looks on. We also see enslaved people milling about the scene as if Northup is not there, until one gives him some water to drink. As the audience steels itself for Northup's death, we let out a collective breath of relief as the master cuts him down from the tree. The viewer comes away with a hatred of yeoman, men whose unveiled hatred of enslaved men and women reveals their own status insecurities; a distaste for overseers, not for protecting Mr. Northup from the yeoman and fellow overseers, but for failing to protect him from the noose; gratefulness for the master who seeks to transfer Northup from harm's way even as he speaks of his own economic preservation; and a sense of sorrow for Mr. Northup who has been relinquished to the horrors of slavery though once ebulliently and magnificently free. Yet and still, these events freeze in time the complex relationship between the plantation owner (planter/enslaver), overseer, yeoman, and the enslaved. The moment reveals that the slave South, a region characterized by commoditized land and labor, was not solely a society polarized by race, White people against Black people. Rather, it was a society where not all White men were afforded the same rights and privileges presumed to be firmly attached to all White males living in southern antebellum society.

The work of race and masculinity scholars has done much to advance our understanding of the bundled identities of White males.[16] In unpacking this bundle, scholars of race have revealed that "whiteness" consists of social, economic, and political privileges that change according to time, region, and social context. While it is common to speak of the bundle in its totality as "race" +"class" + "gender," such labels obfuscate the multiple interlocking parts that create them, namely white supremacy, patriarchy, and capitalism. At their core race and gender are classifications of people by appearance, but also much more. Each classification bestows upon those grouped within it various access points to social, political, and economic benefits. In much the same way, class, as Rita Mae Brown describes it in her essay "The Last Straw," "involve[s] [a person's] behavior, [their] basic assumptions, how [they] [were] taught to behave, what [they] expect from [themselves] and others, [their] concept of a future, how [they] understand problems and solve them, [and] how [they] think, feel, act."[17] When viewed in this manner, class is simultaneously a social construction and a material determination derived from capitalism.[18] Race and gender, like class, are simultaneously social constructions and means of conveying material benefits according to contextually derived hierarchies ordered by white supremacy and patriarchy.

Gender operates within patriarchy as "a specific system of exchange that arose in the context of modern capitalism."[19] Masculinities are performances of gender that are assigned value based on the imperatives of capitalist and white supremacist structures. Writ large, they are "configurations of practice that are accomplished in social action, and therefore, can differ according to the gender relations in a particular setting."[20] As accomplished in the social action of employment relationships between planters and overseers, masculinities configured in the professional practices of these men required whiteness and maleness as access points for ownership of land and enslaved labor in the plantation economy. In this particular setting, white supremacy and patriarchy converged to create a hegemonic masculinity defined by the characteristics of the planter elite. As sociologist and masculinity scholar R. W. Connell explains, "Hegemonic masculinity is not a fixed character type, always and everywhere the same. It is, rather, the masculinity that occupies the hegemonic position in a given set of gender relations."[21] Connell along with fellow sociologist James Messerschmidt goes on to explain that "at a local level, hegemonic patterns of masculinity are embedded in specific social environments, such as formal organizations."[22] The formal organization in which the masculinities discussed in this book are embedded is the plantation.

Overseer contracts, plantation management manuals, and overseer correspondence with planters are insufficient alone to tell us how White men experienced, talked about or argued about what whiteness and maleness meant or should have meant. Nevertheless, these items provide us a window into how their employment relationship was the context in which each negotiated their whiteness and maleness while navigating the terrain of the plantation and consequently the plantation economy. Antebellum society in large measure defined people by what they did. Planters owned the enslaved people and land that made plantations, and overseers managed enslaved labor and plantation land. These "job descriptions" also carried race, class, and gender characteristics. Planters were White, upper class, and primarily male persons, and overseers were White men who worked for planters and were members of poor White society. These distinctions are important for several reasons. Planters could attempt to manipulate through contracts, public and private law, and plantation management systems what aspects of their bundled identities overseers could access. Through these mechanisms, they could determine exactly how much significance society would ascribe to the whiteness and maleness possessed by their race unequals—overseers. The circumscription of overseers' social and economic spaces by the terms of their employment restricted their ascent into the upper classes, and consequentially, the gendered racial hierarchy as well. Minimal opportunities for overseers' economic upward mobility determined how their race, class, and gender were constructed at the hands of the planters who drafted their employment contracts—contracts that carefully mediated the tension between ownership and managerial control of the land and enslaved.

Enslavers, both in and outside of the plantocracy or planter elite, were a highly fluid class of persons comprising those seeking a chance at upward mobility.[23] However, this mobility excluded enslavers who owned five enslaved persons or less.[24] At the very top of this class pyramid were planters or those White male elites who owned twenty enslaved persons or more. Although planters were the smallest percentage of all enslavers, they were the wealthiest within the wealthiest class.[25] They were the proverbial 1 percent. Like the yeoman and poorer classes of White people in the antebellum south, planters and small-scale enslavers were united by the twin goals of owning land and enslaved labor, which characterized the pinnacle of achievement and the benchmark of independence.[26] As Stephanie McCurry underscores in *Masters of Small Worlds: Yeoman Households, Gender Relations, and the Political Culture of the Antebellum South Carolina Low Country*, although planters and yeoman both defined themselves by the property and dependents they controlled, they were not equals. Of South Carolinian societal relationships, both on and outside the plantation, she writes:

> Domestic dependencies had public meanings in the South Carolina Low Country. In the complex world outside the fence where masters met on no man's

particular land, yeoman's masterly identity engendered quite contradictory meanings, committing them to independence and the public assertion of their social and political rights even as it wedded them to the relations of power and domestic dependency [plantation life and society] that supported it.[27]

In the wide spectrum of class occupied by White people living in the antebellum south, the economic dimensions of class had many social implications.

Despite the obvious economic divisions among planter/enslavers, non-slave holders, and yeoman, race among them (whiteness) was defined by each group's ability to own property (land and slaves).[28] Access to property assured planters and yeoman alike independence over their own affairs, and freedom from dependence on others. Dependence was associated with the African enslaved, who could in no way be the equals of White people, despite any access to economic resources.[29] However, while there were certain "rights" of whiteness, namely land and slave ownership, mechanisms in society (e.g., contracts and public and private law) restricted large-scale property ownership to the wealthier class of White persons and shuffled managerial control of that property to White persons outside of their ranks. Thus, whiteness itself was gendered—it was defined by the White male accoutrement of upper-class economic status derived from ownership of enslaved labor.[30] This whiteness and its regulation of relationships between independent and dependent plantation employees did not guarantee economic or social equality to all southern antebellum White males.

This book is about one segment of these relationships, the employment relationship between White planters and White overseers. The labor ties between these two groups of White men solidified planters' class position and aided in defining the White masculinities upon which southern antebellum society was built. The duties of the overseer, maintained by a complex web of private law (contracts), public law (legislation), and plantation management manuals, preserved planters' status in two main ways. First, planters' inconsistent, inadequate, or non-payment of wages to overseers limited their access to land and enslaved labor—two items that defined the ideal whiteness, or the "elite" whiteness of planters in the antebellum south. Second, obligations imposed by law and overseers' contracts placed limitations on how overseers allocated their own time and labor. These constraints placed them in a position of economic, gender, and racial inferiority to planters. Overseers' restricted control over their bodies and its benefits aided in defining their whiteness and maleness, their White masculinity, as something less than their planter counterparts.

Contract terms and plantation management manuals placed many responsibilities on the overseer. His management or mismanagement of the plantation was a significant factor in the planter's economic fate. The overseer was legally obligated to fulfill the terms of his contract, which placed good management of the plantation first, or risk termination. Because a favorable return on the crops would increase a planter's economic status, the overseer was integral to the planter's acquisition of wealth. Paradoxically, the overseer's fulfillment of his duties limited his own upward mobility. Moreover, terms of overseers' contracts and directives in plantation management journals also urged and in some cases compelled the overseer to follow a complex code of social behavior that proved his seriousness to his job and his morality to his planter employer. The latter case provided planters with the tools to define the boundaries of appropriate social behavior for overseers, which, in turn, set him apart as the "other" within his own race and its male elite.

Over five chapters, this study examines the contractual relationships between overseers and planters, and their role in shaping managerial identity in southern antebellum society. Chapter 1, "The Overseer, His Contracts, and His Contractual Relationships," introduces the overseer, how he offered his labor in the plantation market economy, and the significance of overseer employment contracts as a form of labor regulation for non-elite White male bodies in the antebellum south. Chapter 2, "Profitable Planters, Industrious Overseers, Maintaining the Status Quo," explores how contractual arrangements limited overseers' upward economic mobility by failing to facilitate the regular and consistent payment of promised wages. It also examines how litigation over nonpayment of wages placed overseers in greater financial peril, while enforcing planter protection of their financial assets. Chapter 3, " 'Pushing' Torture, Managing Violence, and Planter Regulation of Overseer Control," considers the managerial components of the "pushing system" of labor, the purpose of which was to maximize enslaved labor productivity and ultimately planter wealth. It further interrogates the interlocking nature of public law (legislation), private law (overseer contracts), and common law (litigation interpreting both) in creating duties and obligations for planters and overseers in the field of plantation management. Chapter 4, "White Masculinities, Private Law, and the Battle for Social Control," places overseer employment contracts at the center of the planters' fight to block overseer access to their status as elite White men. Planters used their contracts with overseers as a means of social control. These contracts served as rulers to measure the point at which overseer access to land and enslaved labor crossed the boundary to threaten planters' elite White male identity. Planters then set them as boulders, blocking the gateway to overseers' upward mobility as White men and laborers in the plantation economy. Chapter 5, "Immoral Men, Immoral Ends, Deference as Social Death," explores how litigation concerning overseer employment contract terms outlined the scope of planter duty and the limits of overseer authority in plantation management. As fought out in the courts, planter duty was an expression of elite White male identity.

That planters transferred to overseers authority to help them fulfill their duties as landowners and enslavers reveals that overseers were not the same "type" of White men. Reinforcing this notion were morality clauses in overseer contracts. Through them, planters regulated overseers as the baser sort of White males, a popular social perception of overseer identity.

The overseers that are the subject of this study were located on cotton plantations in Alabama, Arkansas, Georgia, Mississippi, and Louisiana on which there was a workforce of twenty or more enslaved. Cotton plantations are significant in the plantation economy, because cotton produced in the United States was a basis for its domination of the global economy throughout the majority of the nineteenth century.[31] As historian Sven Beckert describes in his book *Empire of Cotton: A Global History*, "new cotton fields sprouted in the sediment rich lands along the banks of the Mississippi, the upcountry of Alabama, and the black prairie of Arkansas. By the 1830's Mississippi produced more cotton than any other southern state."[32] Historian Edward E. Baptist echoes in his *The Half Has Never Been Told: Slavery and the Making of American Capitalism*, "[by] 1819, the rapid expansion of Mississippi Valley slave labor camps enabled the United States to seize control of the world export market for cotton, the most crucial of the early industrial commodities."[33] Although historians and economists have varied opinions about the centrality of cotton as a commodity in driving U.S. economic development, what is certain is that the deadly combination of Native American land divestment, expansion of cotton plantations throughout the Southwest, and the trade and enslavement of the millions of Africans that resulted advanced the forward march of global capitalism.[34] The five collections that are the focus of this study are as follows: Jackson and Prince Family Papers 1839–1843 (Alabama and Georgia); James Sheppard Papers 1830–1889 (Hanover County, Virginia, Copiah County, Mississippi, and Jefferson County, Arkansas); Haller Nutt Papers 1846–1860 and Journal of Araby Plantation 1846–1850 (Mississippi and Louisiana); Joseph M. Jaynes Plantation Journals 1854–1860 (Rankin County, Mississippi); and the Samuel O. Wood Papers 1847–1865 (Marengo County, Alabama—Tarry Plantation). Data from these holdings give us a glimpse of how relationships between planters and overseers evolved on plantations that were most likely to require overseer (managerial) labor.

Other characteristics also make these sources rich for the study of overseers. As a result of their wealth, each planter owned more than one plantation and traveled extensively back and forth between them. Due to their absence from one or more plantations at any given time, correspondence with overseers and/or extensive records of work performed on the plantation was a necessary evil. The correspondence and records give us a snapshot of day-to-day plantation life.

The collections also provide various lists of enslaved persons, work journals, planters' tax returns, yearly values of crops, overseers' contracts, plantation rules governing overseers, and portions of plantation management journals. These sources show that running a large plantation was an extensive managerial undertaking. The varied nature of sources allows for cross-referencing information that is found in each one, which attests to the validity of the information reported. Also, these sources aid in determining how employment relationships between overseers and planters were structured and implemented, and the implications for the roles each were allowed to play in southern antebellum society.

Lastly, public law (legislation) and litigation interpreting legislation and contract terms (private law) are important parts of this study. Initially, I pulled more than 800 cases involving criminal and civil litigation over enslaved labor, the plantation, overseers, and planters. I sorted them according to allegations of overseer mismanagement with respect to: punishing the enslaved; attending to enslaved health concerns; attending to the crops; and otherwise fulfilling the obligations of plantation management. This produced a yield of approximately 140 cases. Because the plantations that are the focus of this study are located in Alabama, Arkansas, Georgia, Mississippi, and Louisiana, the cases discussed throughout are located there also. Of the approximately 140 cases, about 90 were from these states, and 40 or so made it into this study.[35] Additionally, I pulled statutes from Alabama, Arkansas, Georgia, Mississippi, and Louisiana regulating the general treatment of enslaved persons, surveillance of enslaved labor on plantations, enslaved labor and public works, and other laws about plantation management broadly construed. Together, the cases and statutes provide a dynamic context in which to interpret the role of overseer contracts and plantation management schemes in building White masculinity and managerial identity in the plantation economy.

NOTES

1. Solomon Northup, *Twelve Years A Slave* (2009), 43, Kindle.
2. Ibid., p. 44.
3. Ibid., p. 43.
4. Ibid., pp. 46–47.
5. Ibid., p. 41.
6. Ibid., pp. 44–50.
7. Ibid., p. 44.
8. Ibid., pp. 44–45.
9. Ibid., p. 46.
10. Ibid., pp. 46-47.
11. Ibid., p. 47. Emphasis mine.

12. Ibid., p. 49. Northup surmised that Chapin left him hanging for one of two reasons. Either he wanted Ford to see the damage that Tibeats, Cook, and Ramsay did to him, or Chapin was afraid that Tibeats would have brought trespassing charges against Chapin for handling Northup (Tibeats' property).

13. Ibid., pp. 47–49.
14. Ibid., pp. 49–50.
15. Ibid., pp. 50–51.
16. See Janet E. Helms, *Black and White Racial Identity: Theory, Research and Practice* (Westport: Praeger Publishers, 1990) (developing a model for white identity formation in historical context); David R. Roediger, *The Wages of Whiteness: Race and the Making of the American Working Class* (New York: Verso, 1991) (discussing how European ethnicities assimilated into whiteness in the context of white supremacy and its role in forming the working class); Christine Clark and James O'Donnell, eds., *Becoming and Unbecoming White: Owning and Disowning a Racial Identity* (Westport: Praeger Publishers, 1999) (a critical pedagogy primer for anti-racist education); Ronald L. Jackson II, *The Negotiation of Cultural Identity: Perceptions of European Americans and African Americans* (Westport: Praeger Publishers, 1999), xiv, 8 (exploring the development of intracultural identity among African Americans and European Americans, respectively); David R. Roediger, ed., *Colored White: Transcending the Racial Past* (Berkeley: University of California Press, 2002) (charting the history of white identity formation in the United States); Kath Woodward, ed., *Questioning Identity: Gender, Class, Ethnicity* (New York: Routledge, 2004) (unpacking identity formation in the United Kingdom by examining race, gender, class, ethnicity and nationhood); Jennifer Ritterhouse, *Growing Up Jim Crow: How Black and White Southern Children Learned Race* (Chapel Hill: University of North Carolina Press, 2006) (a study of "racial etiquette" and its role in white identity formation in the segregated south); George Lipsitz, *The Possessive Investment in Whiteness: How White People Profit from Identity Politics* (Philadelphia: Temple University Press, 2006) (arguing that "public policy and private prejudice work together to create a 'possessive investment in whiteness' [a derived economic benefit from access to opportunity and power] that is responsible for the racialized hierarchies of our society"); Kristina Durocher, *Raising Racists: The Socialization of White Children in the Jim Crow South* (Lexington: The University Press of Kentucky, 2011) (exploring the race and gender dimensions of acculturating white southern children into a white racial identity); Matthew E. Hughey, *White Bound: Nationalists, Antiracists and the Shared Meanings of Race* (Stanford: Stanford University Press, 2012) (examining white racial identity formation within antiracist and nationalist frameworks).

17. Seebell hooks, *Feminism is for Everybody: Passionate Politics* (London: Pluto Press, 2000), 39.

18. Ibid., p. 39.

19. R. W. Connell and James Messerschmidt, "Hegemonic Masculinity: Rethinking the Concept," *Gender & Society* 19, no. 6 (December 2005), 839.

20. Ibid., p. 836.

21. Hugh Campbell, Michael Mayerfeld Bell & Margaret Finney, "Masculinity and Rural Life: An Introduction," in *Country Boys: Masculinity and Rural Life*, Hugh

Campbell, Michael, Mayerfeld Bell & Margaret Finney, eds. (University Park, The Pennsylvania State University Press, 2006), 10.

22. Connell and Messerschmidt, "Hegemonic Masculinity: Rethinking the Concept," 839.

23. James Oakes, *The Ruling Race: A History of American Slaveholders* (New York: W.W. Norton & Company, 1998), 39, 58-59.

24. Oakes, *The Ruling Race*, 40, 58–59. Oakes defines middle-class enslavers as those who held other careers in addition to occupying positions as masters. For a similar discussion, see Lacy K. Ford, Jr., *Origins of Southern Radicalism: The South Carolina Upcountry 1800–1860* (New York: Oxford University Press, 1988), 70-73.

25. Oakes, *The Ruling Race*, 41.

26. Ibid., 76–77, 123; Stephanie McCurry, *Masters of Small Worlds: Yeoman Households, Gender Relations, and the Political Culture of the South Carolina Low Country* (New York: Oxford University Press, 1995), 92, 107–108; Ford, *Origins of Southern Radicalism*, 72–74. By this observation, I do not mean to imply that planter/enslavers were solely driven by the acquisition of material goods. However, many of their relationships within their households and with other classes of White people stemmed from the very acquisition of those goods. For example, planters extended credit, the use of their farming equipment, and provided plantation jobs for poorer classes of White persons. However, the foundation of these relationships was the planter's acquisition and possession of wealth, which, in turn, created these social expectations (expectations that he would extend these services) for the less fortunate of the community. See Drew Gilpin Faust, *James Henry Hammond and the Old South: A Design for Mastery* (Baton Rouge: Louisiana State University Press, 1982); Charles C. Bolton, *Poor Whites of the Antebellum South: Tenants and Laborers in Central North Carolina and Northwest Mississippi* (Durham: Duke University Press, 1994).

27. McCurry, *Masters of Small Worlds*, 92.

28. Oakes, *The Ruling Race*, 134; Ford, *Origins of Southern Radicalism*, 50–51.

29. Ford, *Origins of Southern Radicalism*, 50–52.

30. Oakes, *The Ruling Race*, 52. Oakes states "[to] own twenty slaves in 1860 was to be among the wealthiest men in America, easily within the top five percent of southern white families. Barely one and twenty slaveholders owned that many bondsmen and not one in a hundred southern white families was headed by such a man. Yet southern white society is frequently analyzed from the perspective of this tiny elite."

31. Sven Beckert, *Empire of Cotton: A Global History* (New York: Vintage Books 2014); Edward E. Baptist, *The Half Has Never Been Told: Slavery and the Making of American Capitalism* (New York: Basic Books, 2014), 82–83.

32. Beckert, *Empire of Cotton*, 103.

33. Baptist, *The Half Has Never Been Told*, 82–83.

34. For example, Calvin Shermerhorn, *The Business of Slavery and the Rise of American Capitalism* (New Haven: Yale University Press, 2015), 2. The authors argue that "North American capitalism developed in the context of an Atlantic system of exchange most recognizable perhaps in the transatlantic slave trade and the systems of indebtedness responsible for its contours." Kathryn Susan Boodry, "The

Common Thread: Slavery, Cotton, and Atlantic Finance from the Louisiana Purchase to Reconstruction." (PhD diss., Harvard University, 2014), 11, 15–16 (linking cotton cultivation, production, and export to the growth of Western capitalism). For criticisms of the key theses in Baptist and Beckert's work, see Alan L. Olmstead and Paul W. Rhode, "Cotton, Slavery, and the New History of Capitalism," *Explorations in Economic History* 67 (2018), 12–13. The authors argue that "[Baptist and Beckert] vigorously advance the idea that the Cotton South drove national expansion. They fail to mention that this hypothesis has been proposed, rigorously tested, and rejected several times."

35. For more on the development of the common law of slavery in Arkansas, see L. Scott Stafford, *Slavery and the Arkansas Supreme Court*, 19 U. Ark. Little Rock L.J. 413 (1997).

Chapter 1

The Overseer, His Contracts, and His Contractual Relationships

THE OVERSEER

The varied classes of White men and women that worked and resided in the antebellum south often defy categorization. With few exceptions, White skin was a prerequisite for owning Black bodies, but many White men and women were excluded from this privilege because of the White bodies into which they were born. However, this does not mean that White men and women were removed from the rights, responsibilities, and privileges that birth into any White body bestowed. The wealth of the plantation economy was part of a broader system of capitalism buttressed by racial caste, class position, and gender subjugation. Southern antebellum society was a society stratified by these same interlocking systems that brought oppression for some and elevation for others.

White men and women in this society labored in various positions reflective of the access points to capitalism granted by their race, class, and gender. In the most incisive and comprehensive study of White wage laborers in southern antebellum society to date, historian Keri Leigh Merritt casts the whole of this group—inclusive of "white tenants, croppers, day laborers, and [mechanics]"—as "non-slaveholding" and "poorwhite".[1] Merritt sets these laborers as collateral damage to the system of enslavement, which limited their employment opportunities and drove down their wages at best, or made the need for their labor superfluous at worst.[2] They owned neither land nor enslaved labor, but stood a cut below farmers who owned both, and far below the planter-architects of the plantation economy responsible for their abysmal economic station.[3] For Merritt, overseers are not part of the categories of non-slaveholding and poor White people, despite owning neither property nor slaves. They are marginal to the author's study, mentioned only once and described as far beyond the category of the White non-slaveholding poor.[4] Merritt writes:

> To understand fully the working lives of poor white men in the Deep South, a persistent myth must first be dispelled. While many historians assume that the ranks of overseers were filled with poor white men, this supposition is simply incorrect. Overseers generally came from the yeomen or middling classes. Sometimes the younger sons of affluent slaveholders spent parts of their early adulthoods learning to manage slaves, buying time until they could purchase their own land and slaves or acquire them through inheritance. Overseers were paid well, and salaries that high would have priced a poor white out of the lower classes and into the middling classes. Furthermore, few poor men would have had the opportunity for employment as an overseer in the first place, because the vast majority of overseers needed to know how to read and write, and many were required to have basic math skills. As one of the WPA [Works Progress Administration] interviewers wrote, a good overseer was "supposed to have an education, so that he could handle the finances of the plantation accurately, and to be possessed of a good moral character." The average pay "was from three to five hundred dollars a year." Taking the lowest figure, even $300 a year comes out to $25 a month, about twice as much as a poor white laborer could expect to earn if he found full time employment.[5]

Merritt's description of overseers comes from only one source,[6] which perpetuates many preconceptions about overseers that are otherwise false. This facile treatment of overseers does not adequately deal with them as a subcategory of wage earners among southern White male labor in the antebellum period.

The majority of Merritt's poor White people and all of the overseers that occupy the pages of this text were White men; all were laborers, and all were impacted differently by the plantation economy. As uneducated, non-slaveholding wage laborers, Merritt's category of poor Whites' means to make money was undermined primarily by enslaved agricultural labor. Overseers were literate, not necessarily educated,[7] non-slaveholding, salaried wage earners whose work supported the plantation economy and the dominance of enslaved agricultural labor. Both groups were White men, but neither group was planters. Overseers were not in direct competition with enslaved labor, but facilitated the economy that also limited their access to the pinnacle of White maleness—planters who owned land and enslaved labor—and the wealth that status bestowed. Because of their Whiteness and maleness, "poor whites" and overseers had the right to offer their labor freely. However, various degrees of literacy, numeracy, and the ability to implement plantation management schemes determined the monetary and societal value of their whiteness and maleness in the plantation economy.

Admittedly there is not much secondary literature about overseers, but what exists suggests that for them the nature of their work on southern antebellum plantations was consistent, if not constant. William Kauffman Scarborough's *The Overseer* has offered the most well-known scholarship on overseers.[8] Scarborough wrote in direct opposition to scholars before him that characterized the overseer as inept in his work. Such literature dominated the scholarship. A more nuanced reading of Merritt's assertion—that the enslaved's references to overseers as poor white trash were "simply meant to degrade the overseer, demeaning his character and reputation by comparing him to 'mean' and 'low' whites—by deeming him trash,"[9]—reveals that common perceptions of overseer reputations were a social currency used to reify the supremacy of planter's White manhood.[10] For example, Lewis Gray wrote in his *History of Agriculture in the Southern U.S.* that overseers were "unreliable and dishonest, and in their treatment of slaves, cruel, drunken and licentious tyrants."[11] He went on to say that many complaints about overseers by planters could be found in the contemporary agricultural literature. In Gray's account, even George Washington complained about the behavior of his overseers, citing their lack of skill at being good farmers and their inability to successfully manage the slaves.[12] Similarly, *Advice among Masters*, edited by James O. Breeden, which is a collection of planters' correspondence to each other, contains many observations of overseers' ignorance and inability to be successful managers.[13] Thus, it is readily apparent that until Scarborough's study, the history of overseers was written from the opinions that planters held toward them and not the overseers' views of themselves and their place in plantation society.[14]

The job of overseer meant more than just a commitment to the well-being of the plantation. Overseership was a gateway into a class of manager/wage earners that were not highly regarded outside of the yeoman class and poorer classes of whites.[15] Even among these groups, overseership was a direct threat to the independence that they relished. As Lacy Ford states in *Origins of Southern Radicalism*, "The yeoman farmer feared the fall from independent producer to dependent proletarian, a status he equated with enslavement."[16] Societally, the duties of overseers (e.g., the care and management of the enslaved, supervision of crop cultivation and harvest, and care of animals) were regarded as a base occupation.[17] Becoming an overseer meant entrance into a class of wage earners who facilitated the plantation economy and operated to secure and continue planter wealth, as well as their economic and social dominance.

HIS CONTRACTS

The wealth of the plantation economy was tied to land ownership and its cultivation by enslaved labor. From 1783 to 1861, the ranks of the enslaved increased fivefold.[18] Their labor crowned cotton king and planters extended its coronation to make capitalism sovereign.[19] Planters bought, owned, and sold the bodies of enslaved Africans, but entrusted the management of this labor force to overseers. Overseers' entrance into the plantation economy as salaried wage earners was through employment contracts, which as legal instruments departed sharply in theory and practice from those used to regulate the plantation economy.

In his definitive work *The Historical Foundations of Modern Contract Law*, historian Morton Horwitz argues that modern contract law began in the late eighteenth/early nineteenth century with the emergence of English and American commodities markets.[20] Prior to this time, the title or property theory of contracts—the idea that a contract was an instrument that transferred title to a particular thing—dominated contract law. Horwitz fixes the critique of the title theory of contracts that would lead to alternate theories of contract better suited to the market economy in John Joseph Powell's *Essay Upon the Law of Contracts and Agreements* published in 1790.[21] Of Powell and his progeny, Horwitz wrote, "a major feature of contract writing has been its denunciation of equitable conceptions of substantive justice as undermining the 'rule of law'."[22] Powell espoused the view in his *Essay* that remedies in law and equity for breaches of contract were inconsistent, because the judges who adjudicated contract disputes were different, and the theories of justice each utilized in reasoning through the disputes were different.[23] Arguably, judges who arrived at equitable remedies had more flexibility to decide what would be equitable and just given the parties and the facts for a particular cause of action.[24] In contrast, common law judges were boxed in by precedent, which limited their ability to "do justice" regardless of the parties involved or the facts presented.[25] Powell explained "the rules of law and equity cannot be guided by fallibility of men; it would be destructive to the interest of community that they should."[26] Accordingly, justice at common law "[depended] upon certain and fixed principles of law, and not upon rules and constructions of equity, which when applied there, must be arbitrary and uncertain, depending, in the extent of their application, upon the will and caprice of the judge."[27]

To illustrate this point, Powell used an example of a person who wished to recover a debt against a married woman by suing her, thereby implicating any real and personal property she may have.[28] Under the law of contract, recovery against the woman is not legally possible because she is married and (in the eighteenth century) subject to the laws of coverture—"a femme couvert can have no legal property, and has lost all ability to contract."[29] Powell continues his example, which ends in his conclusion that a legal remedy is not equitable for the married woman, and an equitable remedy for the claimant is not likely forthcoming.[30] It is illuminating that Powell would draw an example of the shortcomings of equity in addressing commercial interests from William Blackstone's Commentaries on the Laws of England.[31] Located just prior to the laws governing husband and wife is the section devoted to master and servant, inclusive of the enslaved.[32]

For Horwitz, this change in thought about contracts was integral to the development of laws governing the sale of goods, how those laws described commerce in goods, and how courts would eventually interpret those laws.[33] He writes:

> In a market, goods came to be thought of as fungible; the function of contracts correspondingly shifted from that of simply transferring title to a specific item to that of ensuring an expected return. Executory contracts, rare during the eighteenth century, became important as instruments for "futures" agreements; formerly, the economic system had rested on immediate sale and delivery of specific property. And, most importantly, in a society in which value came to be regarded as entirely subjective and in which the only basis for assigning value was the concurrence of arbitrary individual desire, principles of substantive justice were inevitably seen as entailing an "arbitrary and uncertain" standard of value. Substantive justice, according to the earlier view, existed in order to prevent men from using the legal system in order to exploit each other. *But where things have no "intrinsic value," there can be no substantive measure of exploitation and the parties are, by definition, equal. Modern contract law was thus born staunchly proclaiming that all men are equal because all measures of inequality are illusory.*[34]

In this context, the value of goods for the sale of which the parties contract is not fixed, but dependent upon what the market will bear at any given time. The fluctuating nature of the market prevents laws regulating contracts for the sale of goods from setting any strict equitable standard or remedy in the event of a breach by the parties. Where there is no fixed value, the law cannot properly adjudicate who has been exploited in the bargain or who has done the exploiting. Because, as Horwitz argues, in the marketplace "measures of inequality are illusory," all of the contracting parties are on equal footing at the point they consent to contract.

Strikingly, Horowitz does not link the commodities about which he writes to the plantation economy that produced them. Cotton was the specific commodity, traded on a global scale, responsible for the modern world economy.[35] The parties who contracted for its sale were operating in a market where its value, in quality and quantity, was determined in large measure by the enslaved men, women, and children who planted, cultivated, and picked it. In the nineteenth century, enslaved Africans laboring on plantations in the American South made the United States the world leader in cotton production and commerce.³⁶ Thus, the first contracts that White men entered in the global marketplace were those for the sale, leveraging, and transfer of land and enslaved labor. At the point of sale, none of the contracting parties could know where the inequity would rest—in the skill of the laborers, the richness of the land, or the management acumen of the overseer. At the point of sale, then, the contracting parties were presumed equal in their uncertainty about the benefits or detriments of their bargains. That the theory of contract integral to this economy, the plantation economy, had to undergo a transformation that jettisoned justice as a foundational tenet is not at all surprising. The law of contractual relations, including that governing commercial transactions, needed to be nimble enough to simultaneously transfer a property interest in the enslaved, and allow speculation on their labor productivity, and its resulting commodities, on the world market.³⁷

Slave mortgages are instructive and exemplars of the legal instruments that facilitated operation of the plantation economy. Although they originated in the seventeenth century, their widespread use in the nineteenth century to secure both land and additional enslaved laborers reflected the shift in theories of contract that Horwitz describes.³⁸ Discussed at length in chapter 2, the antebellum south was a credit economy, and mortgages, as credit instruments, were essential for its operation. In the case of Solomon Northup, whose encounters on a cotton plantation began this book, Northup's former owner, William Ford, agreed to a four hundred dollar mortgage on Northup at the time Ford sold Northup to John M. Tibeats, a yeoman/carpenter, in 1842.³⁹ According to Northup, the mortgage is possible because the price his new owner Mr. Tibeats agreed to pay for him (his market value) was more than the debt Ford incurred in buying him (his actual value).⁴⁰ Ford owned Northup as chattel and used him as collateral to secure a four hundred loan on Northup upon his sale.⁴¹ It is this mortgage that saves Northup from lynching at Tibeats' hands;⁴² with Northup dead, Tibeats's mortgage debt for Northup would be cancelled and Ford would be without Northup's body or labor to use as collateral for any further monetary transactions going forward. What necessitated Northup's sale was Ford's inability to pay his debts, including those to Mr. Tibeats for carpentry services on a variety of projects.⁴³ Transactions like these were ubiquitous in the plantation economy. Planters regularly used mortgage instruments, contracts, to secure cash or credit with their enslaved as collateral. When viewed in this manner, the enslaved represented "stored capital,"⁴⁴ the promise of a future monetary return on their bodies, reproductive labor (children), plantation labor, and the commodities they would produce.⁴⁵ Their value as collateral transcended the ups and downs of the plantation economy because their existence, and the debt owed on their bodies and labor, ensured that planters would continue to work the land and take out even more loans to prevent losing the labor that powered their wealth.⁴⁶

Valuing and regulating White overseer bodies, those who would manage the enslaved, was not a similarly easy task. White men were not subject to the ravages of chattel slavery, and their labor was not a commodity. On the contrary, neither their bodies nor labor could be mortgaged—leveraged against the risks inherent in the financial enterprise of the plantation. Overseers were not itinerant wage labors, like the yeoman farmer/carpenter Mr. Tibeats in *Twelve Years a Slave*. Tibeats, described by William Ford's overseer Mr. Chapin as irresponsible and worthless,[47] was hardly the type of laborer, the type of man, with whom a plantation owner would entrust the entirety of his personal wealth. Tibeats and men like him performed various tasks on the plantation for payment, but otherwise had no investment in its overall financial well-being.[48] In contrast, overseers' employment responsibility was for the financial health of the plantation and the management of its enslaved labor to effect peak productivity and monetary return.

HIS CONTRACTUAL RELATIONSHIPS

As the plantation economy traveled into the territory of modern capitalism and began the transformation of legal instruments sufficient to do its bidding, it still carried the baggage of the title or property theory of contract. The title theory of contract is viewed as a pre-market contract theory, as opposed to the will or promise theory of contract that is modern contract law.[49] Overseer labor, long-term labor (Mr. Chapin) versus short-term gig arrangements (Mr. Tibeats), was outside of the market as contextualized by the plantation economy. Overseers were not in direct competition with other wage laboring White men in the way that wage laboring White men were in competition with the enslaved. For the latter, their wages were set by the market as their skill set ran coextensive with the enslaved—both Solomon Northup and Mr. Tibeats were carpenters. White wage labor, gig labor, was replaceable or exchangeable with enslaved labor, which diminished its value.[50] Conversely, overseer labor was not fungible (not readily exchangeable or replaceable) and not measured according to future monetary return.[51] Rather by entering into an employment contract with a planter, an overseer consented to transfer his ownership over his labor for the term of the contract in exchange for a variety of tangible and intangible items to be paid during or at the end of the agreed-upon term.[52]

In his *A Property Theory of Contract*, legal scholar Andrew S. Gold provides a useful framework applicable to the contractual relationships between overseers and planters. Gold argues that a contract operates to transfer the ownership rights one person has in his actions to another.[53] The person to whom the ownership rights are transferred gains a property interest in the future actions of the person who initiated the transfer, provided there is adequate consideration compatible with the contract terms.[54] Foundational to Gold's thesis is that the person who transfers the rights to his actions owns them, and has a property interest in them, to the extent that he can transfer those rights to another.[55] Undergirding this theory is the application of the harm principle in the common law of contracts to deal with actions that infringe upon a person's contractual rights.[56] While contractual breach may necessitate judicial intervention, the range of judicial intervention, or any means of intervention to enforce the contract for that matter, depends on interpretations of the harm that the breach caused the parties to the contract.[57]

Key to understanding how harms may be interpreted contextually is comprehension of the scope of individual rights that a person may transfer by contract.[58] Using an entitlements approach to explain the transfer of individual rights by contract, legal scholar Randy Barnett explains,

> the function of an entitlements theory based on individual rights is to define the boundaries within which individuals may live, act, and pursue happiness free of the forcible interference of others. A theory of entitlements specifies the rights that individuals possess or may possess; it tells us what may be owned, and who owns it; it circumscribes the individual boundaries of human freedom.[59]

The author goes on to contend that

> whether a purported right is genuine or can be legitimately transferred is not an issue of contract theory only, but is one that may also require reference to the underlying theory of entitlements—that is, the area of legal theory that specifies what rights individuals have and the manner by which they come to have them. In this respect, the explanation of the binding nature of contractual commitments is derived from more fundamental notions of entitlements and how they are acquired and transferred.[60]

In the antebellum south, overseers owned the rights to their labor based on their status as White people and as men. These rights were derived from a society stratified by enslaved and free labor, and the racial and gendered meanings attached to both.

Unlike enslaved individuals, an overseer did not relinquish ownership of his body along with his labor. However, what he did relinquish by contract were certain characteristics of his whiteness and maleness, his White masculinity, that would undermine planter primacy in the antebellum south. Overseers were not far from the master class, but they were not part of the master class. They were not slaveholders, but slaveholder adjacent. In a society that defined its inhabitants by what they did, overseer management of plantations and enslaved labor left little to differentiate their White masculinity, their ability to freely give their labor and assume management responsibilities, from the masculinity embodied by the men of the planter class. Overseer contracts functioned as a means of social control to minimize overseers' threat to planters' social standing. Via contract terms, planters transferred their entitlement to full control over their land and enslaved for a time, in exchange for overseer management of their plantations and limited access to their White male patriarchal and race rights. In turn, overseers transferred their labor and societally derived right to the full entitlements of White manhood, hegemonic White masculinity, to planters for a time, in exchange for a salary to manage plantations and limited access to White male patriarchal and race rights. Overseer contracts underscored that the protections of whiteness and White maleness were built on the planter class by devaluing the social and economic status of overseers.

NOTES

1. Keri Leigh Merritt, *Masterless Men: Poor Whites and Slavery in the Antebellum South* (New York: Cambridge University Press, 2017), 4–5.
2. Ibid., pp. 4–5.
3. Ibid., pp. 13–15.
4. Ibid., pp. 84–85.
5. Ibid., p. 84.
6. Ibid., p. 84, n. 41.
7. For example,, Richardson v. Pumphrey, 2 La. Ann. 448 (1847), where the Louisiana Supreme Court found that it was beyond an overseer's education to keep the regular accounting books of the sort used by businessmen. See also Jan Richard Heier, "A Content Comparison of Antebellum Plantation Records and Thomas Affleck's Accounting Principles," *The Accounting Historians Journal* 15, no. 2 (Fall 1988): 138. Heier states "[though] the overseer had primary responsibility of the plantation's day to day record keeping, the planter was to take the responsibility of performing a full inventory and valuation of the [African Americans] that he owned at the end of the year." This act reflects a planter's duty as the owner of his enslaved labor and land, rather than as a manager of them.
8. William K. Scarborough, *The Overseer: Plantation Management in the Old South* (Baton Rouge: Louisiana State University Press, 1966). See also William E. Wiethoff, *Crafting the Overseer's Image* (Columbia: University of South Carolina Press, 2006). Wiethoff's is the first major contribution to the scholarship of overseers since Scarborough's study, upon which it heavily draws. Because Wiethoff's study is more concerned with how overseer reputations were constructed rhetorically and historically to create a particular discourse about slavery, his work is given only brief mention in this book.
9. Merritt, *Masterless Men*, 84.

10. Due to their close working proximity to overseers, it is probable that the enslaved understood that overseers' place in the plantation hierarchy was dependent upon reinforcing planter paternalism. Eugene Genovese and Elizabeth Fox-Genovese, *Fatal Self-Deception: Slaveholding Paternalism in the Old South* (New York: Cambridge University Press, 2011), 52. Reaffirming a planter's place as the benevolent father of the plantation necessarily meant that overseers needed to be cast as "other," a class of White men who worked on the plantation but who were socially located outside of the plantation household. Genovese and Fox Genovese, *Fatal Self-Deception*, 40, 52–53. See also Ariela J. Gross, *"Like Master, Like Man": Constructing Whiteness in the Commercial Law of Slavery, 1800–1861*, 18 Cardozo L. Rev. 263, 265 (1996). Gross argues that "[witnesses] and judges at trial conjured a good master more complicated than merely "the prudent father of the family"; he was a statesmanlike disciplinarian and a smart manager of a plantation—which meant being a shrewd businessman."

11. Lewis Cecil Gray and Esther Katherine Thompson, *History of Agriculture in the Southern U.S. to 1860: Volume I* (Washington, DC: Carnegie Institution of Washington, 1933), 502.

12. Gray and Thompson, *History of Agriculture: Volume I*, 502. For more on planters' dependence on help other than overseers, see William L. Van Deburg, *The Slave Drivers: Black Agricultural Labor Supervisors in the Antebellum South* (Westport: Greenwood Press, 1979), 50–54.

13. James O. Breeden, *Advice among Masters: The Ideal in Slave Management in the Old South* (Westport: Greenwood Press, 1980).

14. Scarborough, *The Overseer*, 13. For a brief introduction to the reasons overseers were treated badly and written about so harshly, see John Spencer Bassett and James Knox Polk, *The Southern Plantation Overseer As Revealed in His Letters* (Northampton: Smith College, 1925), 1–10; James Calvin Bonner, "The Plantation Overseer and Southern Nationalism as Revealed in the Career of Garland D. Harmon," *Agricultural History* 19, no.1 (January 1945): 1–3.

15. William K. Scarborough, "The Plantation Overseer: A Re-Evaluation," *Agricultural History* 38, (January 1964): 13–20, 29, 42. Similarly, Gray states that overseers usually came from the class of small farmers or had previously been mechanics searching for an easier livelihood. He argues that overseers who came from the class of poor whites were a rarity. Gray and Thompson, *History of Agriculture: Volume I*, 502. Gray calls overseership a "'cherished ambition' among poor whites." Gray and Thompson, *History of Agriculture: Volume I*, 486.

16. Ford, *Origins of Southern Radicalism*, 84.

17. Scarborough, "The Plantation Overseer: A Re-Evaluation," 14–15.

18. Baptist, *The Half Has Never Been Told*, xxiii; Schermerhorn, *The Business of Slavery and the Rise of American Capitalism,* 11–12; M. B. Hammond, *The Cotton Industry Part I.: The Cotton Culture and the Cotton Trade* (New York: The Macmillan Company, 1897), 88–89.

19. See E. N. Elliot, ed., *Cotton is King and Pro-Slavery Arguments Comprising the Writings of Hammond, Harper, Christy, Stringfellow, Hodge, Bledsoe, and Cartwright* (Augusta: Pritchard, Abbott & Loomis, 1860); See also Baptist, *The Half Has Never*

Been Told, xxiii; Walter Johnson, *River of Dark Dreams: Slavery and Empire in the Cotton Kingdom* (Cambridge: Harvard University Press, 2013), 291–292.

20. Morton J. Horowitz, "The Historical Foundations of Modern Contract Law," *Harvard Law Review* 87 (1974): 917–918.

21. John Joseph Powell, *Essay Upon the Law of Contracts and Agreements* (London: J. Johnson and T. Whieldon, 1790).

22. Horowitz, "The Historical Foundations of Modern Contract Law," 917.

23. Powell, *Essay upon the Law of Contracts and Agreements*, ix.

24. Ibid.

25. Ibid.

26. Ibid.

27. Ibid., x.

28. Ibid., p. xi.

29. Ibid.

30. Ibid.

31. Sir William Blackstone, *Of Husband and Wife, Commentaries on the Laws of England in Four Books, Book 1, Chapter 15* (London: Banks & Brothers, 1893).

32. Sir William Blackstone, *Of Master and Servant, Commentaries on the Laws of England in Four Books, Book 1, Chapter 14* (London: Banks & Brothers, 1893).

33. Horowitz, "The Historical Foundations of Modern Contract Law," 918.

34. Ibid, 918–919. Emphasis mine.

35. For example, Baptist, *The Half Has Never Been Told*, 113.

36. See Stuart Weems Bruchey, *Cotton and the Growth of the American Economy: 1790–1860: Sources and Readings* (New York: Harcourt, Brace & World, 1967); Edward E. Baptist, *The Half Has Never Been Told*, 113.

37. M. B. Hammond in *The Cotton Industry* writes of this phenomenon:

> " '[the] planter scarcely considers his land as a part of his permanent investment.' It is rather a part of his current expenses. He buys a wagon and uses it until it is worn out, and then throws it away. He buys a plow, or hoe, and treats both in the same way. He buys land, uses it until it is exhausted and then sells it, as he sells scrap iron, for whatever it will bring. It is with him a perishable or moveable property. It is something to be worn out, not improved. The period of its endurance is, therefore, estimated in its original purchase, and the price is regulated accordingly. If it be very rich, level land that will last a number of years, the purchaser will pay a fair price for it. But if it be rolling land, as is the greater bulk of the interior of the southern states, he considers how much of the tract is washed or worn out, how long the fresh land will last, how much is too broken for cultivation, and in view of these points determines the value of the property" 83.

Hammond expounds upon this view with respect to enslaved labor. He explains, "[the] part played by compulsory labor in the cultivation of the cotton plant previous to 1860 was so great as to almost completely identify in the mind of the observer the two institutions, the culture of cotton and negro slavery. . . . The increase in the slave population after 1790 was absorbed mainly by the cotton industry, and we have already noted the wonderful effect which the expansion of this industry had upon the price of slaves" 88–89.

38. Grant Gilmore, *Security Interests in Personal Property* (Boston: Little Brown, 1965), 25; Bikku Kuruvila, *Financialization, Inequality, Stagnation, and Vulnerability in Historical Perspective: Foregrounding the Human Impact of State Policy and the Law from the U.S. to India*, 22 Trinity La. Rev. 1, 13 (2016). Kuruvila describes slave mortgages as part of a complex array of financial instruments necessary for the operation of industrial capitalism. When viewed in the context of financialization, the relationship between law and the financial regulation of markets, the author argues that "financialization is a simply a function of the relative weighting and primacy (not novelty) accorded to financial activities in a given historical moment." Id. at 5-8, 13. Bonnie Martin, "Slavery's Invisible Engine: Mortgaging Human Property," *Journal of Southern History* 76, no. 4 (November 2010): 844–845; 850. Martin notes that in the Virginia, South Carolina, and Louisiana counties that are sampled in her study, slave mortgages increased in the early nineteenth century.

39. Northup, *Twelve Years A Slave*, 43.

40. Ibid.

41. Ibid. It is unclear who was the creditor on Northup's mortgage contract. As Bonnie Martin explains in her article "Slavery's Invisible Engine,"

> "human collateral was used to raise a significant amount of cash and credit; however, the mortgage contracts were dispersed in courthouses and commandants' headquarters across the colonial South, camouflaging the power and scope of the financial engine created. A web of local credit networks anchored by mortgages began to grow in the colonial period. In the nineteenth century, these informal community credit networks expanded. The networks apparently operated alongside, but not directly through, the emerging banking system: banks were used as facilitators and as places for repayment, rather than as primary lenders."
>
> Martin, "Slavery's Invisible Engine," 817, 819.

42. Ibid.

43. Ibid.

44. Seth Rockman, *Scraping By: Wage Labor, Slavery, and Survival in Early Baltimore* (Baltimore: Johns Hopkins University Press, 2009), 234.

45. Peter Depuydt, "The Mortgaging of Souls: Sugar, Slaves, and Speculation," *Louisiana History: Journal of the Louisiana History Association* 54, no. 4 (Fall 2013), 448, 452.

46. Depuydt, "The Mortgaging of Souls," 448, 452–453; Martin, "Slavery's Invisible Engine," 817.

47. Northup, *Twelve Years A Slave*, 47.

48. For example, M. B. Hammond describes these types of White laborers as belonging to "the class of 'poor whites,'" "many of them descendants of the 'redemptioners,' 'servants sold for the custom,' and 'indentured servants' sent into the colonies by Great Britain from the London streets and the debtor prisons. Released from their period of bondage, and finding it impossible to enter the social ranks of the property-holding classes, and with *their labor despised because of the association which it had with slavery*, these people and their descendants had become the parasites of southern society." Hammond, *The Cotton Industry*, 97. See also Wiethoff, *Crafting*

the Overseer's Image, 75–76 (discussing the negativity associated with White men working in close proximity to enslaved labor).

49. Horowitz, "The Historical Foundations of Modern Contract Law," 920.
50. Merritt, *Masterless Men*, 4–5.
51. Horowitz, "The Historical Foundations of Modern Contract Law," 920–921.
52. Andrew S. Gold, *A Property Theory of Contract*, 103 Nw. U. L. Rev. 1, 2–3 (2009).
53. Ibid, p. 13.
54. Ibid.
55. Ibid.
56. Ibid., pp. 9–10.
57. Ibid, pp. 10–13.
58. Barnett, *A Consent Theory of Contract*, 86 Colum. L. Rev. 269, 291–92 (1986).
59. Ibid, p. 291.
60. Ibid, p. 292.

Chapter 2

Profitable Planters, Industrious Overseers, Maintaining the Status Quo

PROFITABLE PLANTERS

With generational wealth,[1] perhaps some luck, and the currency of White patriarchal authority, Dr. Henry Jackson had in his possession at the time of his death in 1840 (and his estate thereafter) no less than 1,412.5 acres of land spread over Clark (520 acres), Appling (490 acres), Muscogee (202.5 acres), and other unnamed counties in Georgia (200 acres).[2] Ten years later, his land would be worth just over $6 per acre (approximately $8,500).[3] While Dr. Jackson and the bulk of his land and enslaved laborers resided in Georgia, he also owned thirty-three additional enslaved men and women who labored at his Cookshay Plantation in Alabama.[4] As of 1840, the enslaved persons at Cookshay were valued at $21,696.[5] The number of enslaved on the Georgia land is difficult to ascertain, but Henry's estate transferred ten of the enslaved from the Cookshay Plantation: John (36), Daphne (27), Mary (12), Emma (10), Eliza (9), Fanny (7), James (6), George (3), Charles (2), and Benjamin (less than one-year-old) to his daughter Sarah to satisfy his bequest to her.[6] Records indicate that the enslaved Sarah owned worked the Georgia land along with approximately twenty to twenty-five enslaved persons by 1852.[7]

The amount of wealth Henry amassed over his lifetime and bequeathed to his wife Martha, their son, Henry, and their daughters, Sarah and Martha, was the result of his land, the enslaved labor, and the overseers who managed both. They ensured that Henry's land and labor produced an acceptable yield. Yet, as Henry and Martha's overseers worked year after year, they could not manage their way into positions as planter patriarchs. Like those employed on the Jackson plantations and elsewhere, overseers may not have been poor vis-à-vis non-slaveholding wage laboring Whites who did not possess the skill set to manage plantation labor. However, overseers did not possess and could not amass planters' assets or their societal currency necessary to translate enslaved labor and land into wealth and membership into the plantocracy.

Henry's assets demonstrate that land and ownership of enslaved labor in the antebellum south were the mainstay of wealth. The plantation was a capitalist undertaking that required a monetary investment in land, enslaved labor, and farm equipment.[8] The money used for plantation start-up costs, such as supplies for residents on the plantations, securing factors to market the crop, and purchasing enslaved labor and agricultural equipment was usually borrowed.[9] Systems of credit in the South were part and parcel of the maintenance of the plantation system.

Future returns on crops and slave labor could be hypothecated, as the system of slave mortgages illustrates. Plainly, money borrowed to obtain crops could be paid back once the crops were sold, and enslaved labor would pay for itself through economic returns on the crop.[10] However, the option of hypothecation was not accessible to small farmers who did not utilize much-enslaved labor or have the means to purchase large parcels of land that would secure an economic return.[11] This placed them at an economic disadvantage because merchants required some assurance that there was sufficient collateral, such as a large crop and sufficient workforce, before giving a year's worth of credit for plantation supplies. Accordingly, the credit system was most favorable to large planters.[12] They alone had access to long lines of credit, opportunities to purchase many parcels of land at once (which almost always guaranteed they would get a good price), and resources to obtain the necessary plantation provisions and agricultural implements.[13] They were also able to ship all of their crops to market at the peak of the season and secure the lowest freight prices.[14]

Although the credit system was most favorable to large planters, its pervasiveness in southern antebellum society cannot be overlooked. The manner by which systems of credit operated between planters and poorer classes of White people was quite complex. Planter employers sometimes compensated yeoman farmers who worked as overseers on neighboring plantations with credit for their labor.[15] This economic arrangement was the antithesis of the ideals of independence and control over property, dependents, and their own labor that yeoman treasured.[16] Yeoman did not wish to hypothecate their own labor or to risk their ability to own land on the fluctuations of the market economy. For this reason, they practiced what historian/economist Gavin Wright calls "safety-first farming," or farming that placed emphasis on diversification of crops.[17] Yeoman's tentative steps into the world of cash crop mono-culture coupled with their inability to access large lines of credit perhaps explain planters' primacy in southern antebellum life. For example, by 1850 in the South Carolina Upcountry and Low Country, those holding property in plantation districts owned 90 percent of the wealth while yeoman and others similarly situated owned less than 5 percent.[18]

Even if yeoman and landless and laboring White people were able to acquire land, laborers were needed for them to receive the most favorable economic return.[19] Families that were large in size had more hands to devote to field and domestic labor, and slave ownership also increased the amount of hands available to make farms as profitable as possible. However, the distribution of enslaved persons among poor White people was not high. For example, although 75 percent of small farmers in the cotton-producing areas of Augusta, Georgia's hinterlands, owned enslaved men and women in the 1860s, they were more likely to own less than five than as many as nineteen.[20] Similarly, in 1850, non-slaveholding yeoman in the South Carolina Upcountry who produced cotton existed in slightly higher percentage (11.0 percent) than yeoman who possessed one to five slaves (10.9 percent). Each produced 1,160 and 1,760 lbs. of cotton, respectively.[21] These numbers suggest that more than five slaves were needed for farmers to make a substantial return on their cotton crops.[22]

The large parcels that comprised Henry's Georgia and Alabama landholdings suggest that land prices could also be a contributor to the failure of small farms. Economic historian Lewis Gray shows that in 1846, the cost of land in Alabama's poor pinelands was $6 an acre.[23] If the costs of the enslaved, animals, and farm implements were added, the cost of a 360-acre farm (which is small by Gray's standards) would require a capital investment of $8,500.[24] Gray further calculated that by 1850, the average acreage per farm was 399.09, and the average value was $2,131.14. With average overseer salaries between $400 and $600 a year on plantations other than sugar, it is unlikely that any overseer could either finance the farm on his own or secure a line of credit necessary to cover the costs.[25]

INDUSTRIOUS OVERSEERS

Historian William Kauffman Scarborough contends that a small percentage of overseers managed to own land and enslaved persons during and after their tenure on the plantations where they worked. On Mississippi and Louisiana cotton plantations, 10 percent of 808 overseers (80.8) owned real property, and 14 percent (113.1) owned on average 3.6 slaves.[26] Scarborough offers no statistics for overseers on cotton plantations in Virginia, North and South Carolina, Tennessee, Alabama, and Georgia. Moreover, his numbers seem somewhat embellished when compared to assessments of poor White men's upward mobility in Augusta's hinterlands. Of the thirty-two men who were manual laborers there (overseers, artisans, laborers, and their sons) in 1850, ten managed to own property by 1860.[27] Although it is impossible to ascertain how many manual laborers were overseers, it is readily apparent that only a few managed to become self-sufficient and independent. Nevertheless, the profession was regarded as a stepping-stone to an independent farming career.[28] Because overseers were furnished with free housing and had to pay only for food and other equipment provided them at the commencement of their contracts, the perceived opportunity to save money was great. Toward this purpose, some overseers allowed planters to hold the balance of their wages after they had settled debts.[29] However, the ideal of overseer independence and self-sufficiency was tediously achieved if at all. Overseers who quit their jobs for independent farming careers often had to return to supplement their income. Furthermore, saving enough money to leave could take many years.[30] If systems of credit in the South, the unavailability of fluid cash, overseers' duties, and payment of wages are taken into account, overseers' failure to advance in large numbers into the ranks of planters comes as no surprise.

The salaries of overseers employed by Martha and Henry Jackson reflect the inconsistency of payment and reveal the unlikelihood that they could buy the large parcels of land or enslaved labor needed to acquire even a marginal return. Several overseers were employed at the Jackson's Cookshay Plantation in Chambers County, Alabama. From plantation book entries and various receipts for payment, it is possible to compare the overseer salaries to yearly cotton profits and to payment practices concerning overseers at Cookshay. Of note in reviewing the profits from cotton production and sales at Cookshay is that this Alabama plantation constituted land in excess of the 1412.5 acres of Georgia land and the thirty or so enslaved that Martha and Henry worked on their Georgia land.

In 1839, on the Cookshay Plantation in Alabama, the return on the cotton crop from January and February cotton sales for 23,806 pounds of cotton was $1,666.23; the overseer, Henry Smith's salary for that year was $500.00.[31] Similarly for the same plantation in 1840, the cotton return was $1,793.00 on 17,355 pounds of cotton, and the overseer's salary due Mr. Henry Smith was again $500.00.[32] In another plantation entry about the 1840 crop, the writer acknowledges that Henry Jackson still owed his overseer Henry Smith the balance of his salary for 1839, which amounted to $446.21 plus interest of $35.68 1/4.[33] Additionally, the Jacksons owed him $206.75 for bacon he had provided for the plantation and another $2.4[7] to satisfy the balance on a small account.[34] Thus, the total amount owed to him by 1840 was 691.07 3/4, the bulk of which was carried over from 1839.[35] In the final note on the overseer's salary, the writer of the entry concluded: "Leaving his [the overseer's] salary for 1840 being $500.00 still due him [and] to bear eight percent interest."[36]

In Henry Smith's case, the possibility of land ownership was precarious at best, because his wages were not dependably dispersed.[37] By the end of 1839, Henry had only received $53.79.[38] The following year, he had only been paid the balance of the amount he was owed for 1839 along with other miscellaneous expenses. Most surprisingly, his salary for 1840 was still owed him by the time the entire cotton crop had been sold and the profits counted. Perhaps the most glaring example of Mr. Smith's unstable economic position is the following receipt from 1843. It read: "The debt due our *former* overseer Henry Smith for the *unpaid balance of his salary for 1838* which was 482.62[?] [and] *with which its accruing interest had amounted to $676.29 was settled with him in the autumn of this year by giving Him a Negro man named Evans.*"[39] Such payment of wages in the form of a single enslaved man, arguably the plantation economy's most valuable commodity, could not have been depended upon to invest in land or additional enslaved labor sufficient to move Smith to planter status.[40]

Between the years 1841–1843 and 1851–1853, comparable characteristics of payment appear. On the Cookshay plantation in 1841 and 1842, the cotton return was $1770.75, and $1798.37[1/2], respectively. The overseers' salaries for these two years were $500.00 for 1841 and $300.00 to Vincent A. Peirson, overseer for 1842.[41] The overseer's salary for 1843 at Cookshay was $275.00 out of a return of $2,172.38. Again in these years, overseers' salaries constituted between 12.7 and 28 percent of the total cotton returns for the years 1841–1843; a small portion of profits from the crops for each of those years for only one Jackson plantation.[42]

By 1852, the Jacksons had yet to ameliorate the manner in which their overseers were paid. In a promissory note written in 1852, Martha Jackson promised to pay the overseer E. B. Whiddon $100.00, with interest being left from December 20, 1851. According to the note, this amount was partial payment of his salary for the year 1851.[43] In January of the following year, Whiddon signed a receipt that acknowledged $50.00 in partial payment of his 1851 salary. By January 1852, he remained partially paid for work he had done in the previous year.[44] Similar to the case of Mr. Smith, Whiddon would not have been in a position to depend on his wages to supplement an investment in land or enslaved labor. An additional document also shows that in the absence of payment for services rendered by Whiddon, necessities such as food were bought on credit and subtracted from his yearly wages.[45] This system of payment ensured that Whiddon would continue to occupy an economic position that remained below his employers. Often times unable to make financial ends meet in his own domestic life, it is unlikely that Whiddon would be able to lay hold of the resources that formed the basis of the plantation economy as an owner and not a laborer.

Although James Sheppard consistently paid the overseers employed at his Waterford Plantation in Arkansas and his Sulpher Springs and Grange Plantations, their salaries remained a small percentage of the overall yearly profits.⁴⁶ Such evidence of these wages can be found in overseer contracts and payment receipts between Sheppard and William A. Collins for employment in 1851 and between Sheppard and David T. Weeks for the same year. Collins contracted for payment of $350.00 for his duties as overseer in 1851, which was paid to him in January of 1852.⁴⁷ In July of 1851, David T. Weeks entered into a contract with James Sheppard for the amount of $33.00/month to "attend to my business during my absence this summer"⁴⁸ For the completion of these services, Weeks was paid $174.98 in January of 1852.⁴⁹ Both salaries comprised only 5.26 percent and 2.63 percent, respectively, of the net profits for 1851.⁵⁰

Four years later, Weeks's salary increased to $625.00 for the year but was only 13.8 percent of the plantation profits.⁵¹ In subsequent years (1856–1858), Weeks's salary was as low as 4.11 percent and as high as 39.46 percent of the cotton profits.⁵² Similarly, the salaries of overseers Robert W. Miller, J. M. Key, and William F. Black, employed by James Sheppard in 1859 and 1860, never rose above 2.22 percent of cotton sales in those years.⁵³ Such low percentages would ensure that employer and employee were not likely to become economic peers.

Many of Sheppard's overseers also found themselves in positions like that of E. B. Whiddon on the Jacksons' Cookshay Plantation. Out of the nine overseers employed by James Sheppard from 1840 to 1860, eight of their contracts required that he (Sheppard) provide some type of food, transportation, or maintenance of transportation for them.⁵⁴ Parker Carradine was provided with meat and bread for his family for the duration of his 1840 contract.⁵⁵ Asa Kemp (1841) was furnished 500 lbs. of meat and bread.⁵⁶ Charles B. Crocker (1844) received 500 lbs. of pork, and a horse to ride.⁵⁷ Thomas E. Senoir (1847) was also furnished food and a horse.⁵⁸ David T. Weeks was provided with bread and a promise by the planter to feed his horse in his 1851 contract. He also received 41 lbs. of meat on credit in the same year, boarding, and a horse to ride in his 1855 and 1856 contracts.⁵⁹ In 1859, Sheppard promised to furnish Robert W. Miller with 500 lbs. of pork, meal for his family, and to feed his horse.⁶⁰ J. M. Key and William F. Black, both overseers in 1860, were supplied with meat and bread for their families, sugar, coffee, a horse to ride, meal, 500 lbs. of meat, and a cow to milk, respectively.⁶¹ All items were provided at the commencement of the contract, and according to its terms the overseers would pay for these provisions when they received their wages.

As these overseers' contracts confirm, overseer salaries were paid at the end of the year with certain household necessities furnished by the planter at the commencement of the contractual term. These necessities were subtracted from the overseers' salary even before the money was paid to him.⁶² Therefore, at the end of the year, the overseer owed money. A letter written by David T. Weeks to James Sheppard serves as an example of the tough financial situation in which overseers could be found. He stated that "the proposition you make to me is no use as I have nothing to buy land with or it wont [sic] suit me the best way to go but I have no money in debt and paying interest."[63] The lack of large amounts of investment capital available during the year of employment made ownership of sufficient land and enslaved labor a distant if not tenuous goal.

MAINTAINING THE STATUS QUO

Overseers fought against the inconsistent or nonpayment of their wages by bringing breach of contract actions against planters. However, in bringing suit, an overseer automatically invited a planter to defend his actions by alleging overseer mismanagement. A court's first determination in these lawsuits was whether the overseer acted competently in managing the plantation. Generally, courts read implied terms into any overseer contract, those being that "[the overseer] is qualified to execute the trust confided in him—that he will diligently superintend the business of his employer—[and] take care and treat the [enslaved] placed under his control with humanity."[64]

An overseer's success in bringing these lawsuits varied from no award of the wages owed to a reduced amount. Several cases handed down by the Louisiana Supreme Court are instructive. The state of Louisiana had a cap of three years on the time that an overseer could work on a particular plantation.[65] In one lawsuit, *Cresap v. Winter*, an overseer worked for six years, but his planter employer refused to pay him.[66] The overseer sued the planter for back wages of $1,000 per year, as well as for $600 for moss that he sold the planter, a total of $6,600.[67] Although the overseer insisted that he was a competent overseer, the planter claimed damages in the amount of $10,000, and alleged that the overseer was "ignorant of the business of managing a plantation, or of an overseer; and that, in consequence of this, his crops were greatly inferior; so much so, that on average, they were not sufficient to pay the expenses of the plantation."[68] The planter also sought reimbursement for money and other items that he advanced to the overseer over his years of employment.[69] The trial court ruled in favor of the overseer, but subtracted the amount of the money and other items that the planter had advanced.[70] The planter appealed, alleging that the three-year cap on overseer employment prevented the overseer from collecting any wages beyond the three-year employment cap.[71] The appellate court reversed the lower court's decision, and lowered the amount it awarded the overseer by $3,000.[72] Adding insult to injury, the court also assessed court costs and the cost of appeal to the overseer.[73]

Garcia v. Garcia was a lawsuit that pitted brother against another.[74] Felix Garcia hired his brother, Carlos Garcia, as an overseer by a verbal agreement between the two.[75] Felix, an agent for Dunlop, Moncure, and Co., was restricted to $8,000 per year as the amount of expenses he could incur on any plantation, as well as to Dunlop, Moncure, and Co. as his sole authorized dealer for plantation supplies.[76] On the verge of a significant financial loss, he subsequently initiated a lawsuit in *antichresis*, or an action to transfer his possession of the plantation and its crops to Dunlop, Moncure, and Co. to satisfy his debt to the company. Carlos had not received his wages as overseer, and in response to Felix's suit physically prevented Dunlop, Moncure, and Co. from removing the crop on the plantation where he worked until he was paid his salary of $1,800 per year and reimbursed for expenses he made in excess of the $8,000 limit.[77] Because Carlos had not entered into a written contract with Felix, the trial court ruled that Carlos was entitled to the lowest amount paid to overseers who did work similar to him.[78] Having decided that amount to be $1,200, the court ordered that Carlos be paid $400, as he had already been paid $800 for services rendered.[79] Further, it did not award Carlos the expenses he had incurred for supplies he purchased from Dunlop, Moncure, and Co.[80] The appellate court reversed the trial court's ruling, but only to allow Carlos reimbursement for expenses.[81] Because neither party objected to the wage amount set by the trial court, it was not adjusted to Carlos's original claim.[82]

Even when set by written contract, the Louisiana Supreme Court reduced the amount of wages agreed upon by the overseer and planter. In *Lambert v. King*, Michael King, was employed by Mrs. Elodie Lambert on her plantation.[83] In 1853, King and Lambert entered into an overseer contract that gave King "exclusive management of the plantation," to do all of the work required on it, and in turn be compensated with a percentage of any sugar or cotton crops that were planted.[84] King worked from November 1853 to August 1854, at which time Lambert fired him on allegations that he mismanaged the plantation and the enslaved labor, and was disrespectful to Lambert.[85] King refused to leave his post or the plantation, and Lambert initiated suit.[86] She asked the court to cancel King's contract, and award her damages in the amount of $2,000.[87] King counter-sued, also asking for $2,000 in damages and that Lambert fulfill the terms of his contract.[88] At trial, the jury ruled in King's favor and awarded him pro-rated wages up to the time he was fired.[89] However, the appellate court reversed the lower court ruling in favor of Lambert, granted her injunction against King, and reduced the amount of wages the jury awarded to King by $250.[90]

Although in these cases overseers did manage to recoup some of that was owed to them, by virtue of their economic precarity they were less able than planters to bear the costs of the litigation. For their trouble, they ran the risk of paying court costs as well, like the overseer in *Cresap v. Winter*. Moreover, the penalty for voluntarily leaving a planter's employ before the end of an agreed-upon contract term was forfeiture of all wages owed under the contract.[91] The overseers who worked on the Jackson and Sheppard plantations exercised wisdom in waiting for their planters to pay them, settling all accounts with payment in enslaved labor, or simply walking away. Overseership was a gamble with an overseer's time and labor against the plantation house and its resources. Using the profession to get ahead proved that in matters of upward mobility, the house always wins.

NOTES

1. The Jackson family was originally from Moreton-Hamstead, Devonshire, England. William O. Foster, Sr., *James Jackson: Duelist and Militant Statesman 1757–1806* 1 (Athens: University of Georgia Press, 2009). His father was a respected member of the Devonshire family. Alexander A. Lawrence, "James Jackson: Passionate Patriot," *The Georgia Historical Quarterly* 34, no. 2 (June 1950): 75–86, 80. Henry's older brother, James Jackson, was Governor of Georgia from 1798 until 1801. Foster, *James Jackson: Duelist and Militant* Statesman, 146. Prior to his gubernatorial term, he served in the House of the first U.S. Congress, and in the Senate for the Third U.S. Congress and after his gubernatorial term. Foster, *James Jackson: Duelist and Militant* Statesman, 69–71, 101, 168–169. During his time in office, he owned enslaved persons and the Cedar Hill Plantation. Foster, *James Jackson: Duelist and Militant* Statesman, 108, 168. Lawrence, "James Jackson: Passionate Patriot," 75–86, 75–76. Henry Jackson had also come from England to establish ties in Georgia. E. Merton Coulter, *Daniel Lee: Agriculturalist: His Life North and South* (Athens: University of Georgia Press, 1972), 110. James had been an early proponent of establishing a state university in Georgia. Lawrence, "James Jackson: Passionate Patriot," 75–86, 76. In 1811, Henry became one of the first professors there, teaching natural philosophy. Coulter, *Daniel Lee*, 110; Schuyler Medlock Christian, "A Sketch of the History of Science in Georgia," *The Georgia Review* 2, no. 4 (Winter 1948): 415–27, 422. He is credited with separating the study of physics and chemistry at the University. Christian, "A Sketch of the History of Science in Georgia," 415–27, 422. After a brief stint in Paris accompanying the U.S Secretary of Legation, Henry returned to Georgia to resume teaching and settled down on his Halscot Plantation near Athens, Georgia (Clark County) from his retirement until his death in 1840. Coulter, *Daniel Lee*, 110.

2. Tax Return of Henry Jackson of Clark County for 1840, JPFP; Tax Return of Henry Jackson of Clark County for 1841, JPFP. It is likely that the 520 acres in Clark County was the site of the Halscot Plantation. Kelly Westfield, "The Enslaved Members of the Davenport Household: Geography, Mobility, and Pre-Davenport House Lived Experiences," (MA Thesis, Georgia Southern University, 2018), 60.

3. M. B. Hammond, *The Cotton Industry*, 84.

4. List of Negroes at the Cookshay Plantation, Alabama 1840, JPFP. By 1847, an overseer contract between Martha J. Jackson, Henry R. Jackson, and Vincent A. Peirson (overseer) for the Cookshay plantation references "[twenty five] working hands, seventeen young children, two old Negroes and two old women not counted with the working hands," for a total of 44 enslaved men and women. Overseer Contract between Martha J. Jackson, Henry R. Jackson, and Vincent A. Peirson, January [19th ?],1847, JPFP.

5. List of Negroes at the Cookshay Plantation, Alabama 1840, JPFP.

6. Codicil to the Last Will and Testament of Doctor Henry Jackson, n.d., JPFP.

7. Ages of Negroes, June 1852, JPFP. The enslaved listed in this document include six enslaved persons in common with the 1840 Cookshay list, List of Negroes at the Cookshay Plantation, Alabama 1840, JPFP. Because those not in common were not documented as enslaved laborers at Cookshay, it is likely that they resided on the Jackson's Georgia land.

8. Gray and Thompson, *History of Agriculture: Volume I*, 302. See also Caitlin Rosenthal, *Accounting for Slavery: Masters and Management* (Cambridge: Harvard University Press, 2018); Baptist, *The Half Has Never Been Told*; Beckert, *Empire of Cotton*; Johnson, *River of Dark Dreams*; Oakes, *The Ruling Race*.

9. Gray and Thompson, *History of Agriculture: Volume I*, 411.

10. Ibid., pp. 409–410.

11. Ibid., p. 410; 489.

12. Ibid., p. 411.

13. Ibid., pp. 479–480.

14. Ibid., p. 480.

15. Ibid., pp. 107–108.

16. Ibid., pp. 92, 107–108. McCurry describes the relationship between yeoman overseers who owned and operated their own farms and planters as "particularly volatile." Ford, *Origins of Southern Radicalism*, 72–74.

17. McCurry, *Masters of Small Worlds*, 64–70; Ford, *Origins of Southern Radicalism*, 73.

18. McCurry, *Masters of Small Worlds*, 93–94; Ford, *Origins of Southern Radicalism*, 71. Ford's statistics on yeoman's wealth only include the Upcountry. He contends that yeoman here produced 20 percent of all cotton. See also Bolton, *Poor Whites of the Antebellum South*, 91, 97. Bolton contends that 10 percent of northeast Mississippi's poor White people in 1850 were able to own land by 1860. The numbers for whites who were tenant farmers and laborers in 1860 were even more dismal. Personal property among tenants averaged $378, and 5 percent of them possessed no personal property. Laborers who were also household heads averaged $158 in personal property, and 20 percent possessed none.

19. McCurry, *Masters of Small Worlds*, 56, 62–64, 70. The author explains that yeoman who had larger families were better off than those who did not. This was, in part, a by-product of "safety first" farming, and the unwillingness of yeoman to use their own labor for wages.

20. J. William Harris, *Plain Folk and Gentry: White Identity and Black Slavery in Augusta's Hinterlands* (Baton Rouge: Louisiana State University Press, 1987),

39–40. Harris argues that rising prices for enslaved labor in the decade before placed them just beyond the small farmers' grasp. Out of these percentages, we can only speculate about the number of small farmers who were also overseers.

21. Ford, *Origins of Southern Radicalism*, 59.

22. Ibid. Ford's table, *Production and Value on Upcountry Farms, 1850* suggests this is true. Middling enslavers, those who owned 6–19 enslaved persons, produced 4,480 lbs. of cotton. Planters, defined as those who owned 20 or more enslaved persons, produced 17,240 lbs. of cotton.

23. Gray and Thompson, *History of Agriculture: Volume I*, 542. Although Gray's calculations may be true of Alabama, his numbers appear somewhat inflated for other southern states during the same time period. Land owned by yeoman in North Carolina's Central Piedmont and in the South Carolina Upcountry was slightly lower. The average price of land in the Central Piedmont was $2.54/acre in 1840, $3.28/acre later in the decade, and $6.05/acre by 1850. In the South Carolina Upcountry in 1850, the value of 73 acres of improved land, the type of farm non-slaveholding yeoman were likely to possess, was $962.80. The farms of slaveholding yeoman (owning 1-5 enslaved persons) were valued at $1,542.10. Despite the lower prices and perceived greater affordability for overseers, the opposite appears to be true. Although credit transactions in the antebellum south were a fixture of the economy, the poor White people of North Carolina's Central Piedmont remained at a disadvantage. Systems of credit were more accessible to the wealthier class of White people who possessed some measure of economic stability. This largely excluded poor White people. Similarly, yeoman's quest to maintain their independence prevented them from becoming too deeply mired in any system of credit.

24. Ibid.

25. Ibid., p. 545; See also M. B. Hammond, *The Cotton Industry*, 93. Hammond places overseer wages at a range of $200–$600 when the planters were onsite and $1,000–$1,500 when the planters were absentee. James Spencer Bassett and James Knox Polk's estimation of overseer salaries ranges from $250 to $600, with $1,000 salaries paid only in special circumstances. *The Southern Plantation Overseer As Revealed in His Letters*, 6.

26. Scarborough, *The Overseer*, 62–64. The author's statistics are somewhat flawed, which he admits. See Ibid., pp. 51–54 (where he explains that his statistics on the number of overseer/enslavers is somewhat distorted). First, all of the overseers he surveyed were not employed. Second, his overseers only come from Hinds, Lowndes, and Yazoo counties in Mississippi and Natihoches Parish in Louisiana. Third, the percentages of enslaved labor and property owned by younger, unmarried men are much lower than the average.

27. Harris, *Plain Folk and Gentry*, 87. It is impossible to trace how many of these men owned real property and enslaved labor in 1850 and 1860 from Harris's statistics. He only traces mobility in these two areas by household heads, but he does not give statistics on what percentage of household heads were manual laborers.

28. Scarborough, *The Overseer*, 29, 41.

29. Ibid., pp. 28, 36.

30. Ibid., p. 47. For example, Alabama overseer John G. Traylor became an independent farmer after fifteen years of overseership. Scarborough contends that a "great number" of overseers were able to achieve land ownership. However, his own research suggests that one important factor had to be present for overseers to own land. This was remaining in the employ of one planter for a significant number of years, as in Traylor's example. This was not as easy as it may appear. Overseer turnover was very high, in part because they were only given a year to prove themselves. Moreover, employment was at will, which meant either contracting party could terminate the employment contract at any time. Ibid., pp. 21–24.

31. Amount of Crops at Cookshay, 1839–1843, JPFP; Amount of Cotton Made in 1839 and delivered in Columbus, Cookshay Plantation Book, JPFP.

32. Amount of Crops at Cookshay, 1839–1843, JPFP; Amount of Cotton Made in 1840 and delivered in Columbus, Cookshay Plantation Book, JPFP.

33. Amount of Cotton made at Cookshay and delivered in Columbus in 1840, JPFP.

34. Ibid. Such reciprocal arrangements were commonplace. As Gray points out, food was one of the perquisites of overseers. Gray and Thompson, *History of Agriculture: Volume I*, 546.

35. Amount of Cotton made at Cookshay and delivered in Columbus in 1840, JPFP.

36. Ibid. Emphasis mine.

37. Scarborough, *The Overseer*, 28. As Scarborough points out, payment for a year's work was commonly dispersed at the end of that year. Although Scarborough also explains that some overseers preferred to leave the credit of their wages, minus minimal funds for necessities, with the planter to facilitate saving, this does not appear to be the case in this instance. In documents discussed in the previous paragraphs, the writer has only noted that the funds were still due to Henry Smith, not that he had subtracted money for necessities and left a credit balance with the Jacksons. Additionally, interest would not be paid on salaries that were being "held" at the overseer's request. This inconsistent payment of wages is not, according to Scarborough, consistent with overseer payment practices throughout the south. However, the court records and plantation documents in this study suggest otherwise.

38. I subtracted the balance of the salary owed him, $446.21 from the amount he was to be paid, $500.00, to arrive at the sum $53.79.

39. Plantation Account Book at Cookshay, 1843, JPFP. Emphasis mine. Evans was twenty-seven by 1843 when he was given to Mr. Smith. List of Negroes at the Cookshay Plantation Alabama, 1840, JPFP. Another document that gives the valuation of enslaved labor for Dr. Henry Jackson's estate (undated) values the oldest enslaved man James who is forty, at $500.00. The enslaved labor decrease in market value as they decrease in age. If this is any indicator of a greater trend that gives older, physically sound enslaved labor a greater monetary value, then Evans at twenty-seven was probably not worth as much as the debt owed to Mr. Smith by the Jackson family. Valuation of Slaves, n.d., JPFP.

40. Bolton, *Poor Whites of the Antebellum South*, 17. Such "payment in kind", as Charles Bolton calls it, was insufficient to facilitate economic prosperity. In the words of a poor White laborer "it would have taken some time and toil for a poor young man

to save enough to buy a farm for some of them had to take trade for their labor." I am also relying on Scarborough and not the particular price of land. As in the case of overseer Traylor, overseers who eventually owned land appeared to save the bulk of their salaries consistently over a period of years, an option that was not available to Smith because he did not receive consistent wages or the bulk of his salary whenever he was paid. Scarborough, *The Overseer*, 47. See also Kirsten E. Wood, *Masterful Women: Slaveholding Widows from the American Revolution through the Civil War* (Chapel Hill: University of North Carolina Press, 2004), 46. Wood discusses Henry Smith specifically and provides even more context for Henry's employment at the Cookshay plantation.

41. Amount of Crops at Cookshay, 1839–1843, JPFP. Cotton Values, 1842–1843, JPFP (names Vincent A. Peirson as overseer).

42. Note: The Jacksons added the overseer's salary into the expenses and subtracted the total amount from the value of the cotton crop to ascertain the profit for that year. By adding in the overseer's salary to the value of the crop minus the other expenses and dividing the overseer's salary by that number, I was able to get the percentage of the overseer's salary. These percentages reflect only this formula, *not* the percentage of the overseer's crop from the raw profit (the value of the crop minus all expenses). The percentage of the overseers salary received when divided by the raw profit would yield much higher numbers. I use the range of percentages *only* to show that the overseer was paid a marginal amount of the yearly cotton returns. For those overseers that percentages are used, there is no contractual arrangement that they were to be paid from a percentage of the crops.

43. Promissory Note by Martha Jackson, 1851, JPFP. I have assumed the writer of the note was Martha since she attended to general administration of the plantation after Henry's death.

44. Receipt to Martha J. Jackson from E. B. Whiddon, January [7th]?] 1852, JPFP.

45. Record of Pork, 1852, JPFP. The document advances 300 lbs. of pork to Whiddon to be deducted from his 1853 salary. See also Overseer Contract between Martha J. Jackson, Henry R. Jackson, and Vincent A. Peirson, 1847, JPFP. Peirson is advanced corn for his family, 300 lbs. of pork, and the use of two milk cows.

46. The overseer correspondence was not always specific about which plantation the letters came from or where the plantations were located. Also, some of Sheppard's plantations are not explicitly named.

47. Overseer Contract between James Sheppard and William Collins, January 23, 1851, JSP.; Payment Receipt, 1852, JSP.

48. Overseer Contract between James Sheppard and D. T. Weeks, July 15, 1851, JSP.

49. James Sheppard in Account with Estate of J. W. Sheppard Deceased, 1850–1852, JSP.

50. Ibid. These records appear to be from the Sulpher Springs Plantation. Although neither overseer contract mentions on which plantation Collins or Weeks was employed, Weeks is named in the Sulpher Springs records as having been supplied meat. Collins is not mentioned in the Sulpher Springs records but the name of Sheppard's agent (W [J?] Butler) who appears on Collins's payment receipt for the balance of the wages

owed him is mentioned. Payment Receipt, 1852, JSP. According to Collins's payment receipt, Sheppard paid the money to Butler to pay to Collins. Payment Receipt, 1852, JSP. Thus, the logical inference is that Collins was also employed at Sulpher Springs.

51. Overseer Contract between James Sheppard and D. T. Weeks, 1855, JSP; Sale 144 Bales Cotton by MacGregor, Alloway, & Co.,1855, JSP.

52. Overseer Contract between James Sheppard and D. T. Weeks, May 27, 1856, JSP; sale of 33 cotton bales by Byrne, Vance & Co for account and risk James Sheppard Esq., 1856, JSP; Plantation Aggregate Accounts, 1857–1858, JSP; sale of 44 cotton bales by Bradley Wilson & Co. for payment of Mr. James Sheppard, 1857, JSP; sale of 80 cotton bales by Bradley Wilson & Co. for account of Mr. James Sheppard, 1857, JSP; sale of 21 cotton bales by Bradley Wilson & Co. for account of Mr. James Sheppard, 1857, JSP; Overseer Contract between James Sheppard and D. T. Weeks, June 17, 1858, JSP; sale of 181 cotton bales by Byrne, Vance & Co. for account and risk James Sheppard Esq., 1858, JSP; sale of 116 cotton bales by Bradley Wilson & Co. for account of James Sheppard, 1858, JSP; sale of 84 cotton bales by Bradley Wilson & Co. for account of Mr. James Sheppard, 1858, JSP. All percentage amounts were gained by adding the amounts of the cotton sales for a particular year and dividing them into the overseer's salary stated in their contract or listed in aggregate plantation accounts. It is impossible to know if the available receipts from cotton sales are all that existed; however, as mentioned previously, the higher the overall profits, the lower the percentage of overseers salaries.

53. Overseer Contract between James Sheppard and Robert W. Miller, February 7, 1859, JSP; Sale of 188 Bales Cotton by Byrne, Vance & Co. for account and risk James Sheppard Esq., 1859, JSP; Sale of 24 Bales Cotton by Byrne, Vance & Co for account and risk James Sheppard Esq., 1859, JSP; Sale of 87 Bales Cotton for account and risk James Sheppard Esq., JSP; Sale of [20 ?] Bales Cotton by Byrne, Vance & Co., 1859, JSP; Sale of 100 Bales Cotton by Bradley Wilson & Co. for account of James Sheppard Esq., 1859, JSP; Overseer Contract between James Sheppard and J. M. Key, July 23, 1860, JSP; Overseer Contract between James Sheppard and William F. Black, April 9, 1860, JSP; Sale of 121 Bales Cotton by Byrne, Vance & Co. for account and risk James Sheppard Esq., 1860, JSP.

54. According to Gray and Thompson, *History of Agriculture: Volume I*, this was quite typical. 546.

55. Overseer Contract, January 2, 1840, JSP.

56. Overseer Contract between James Sheppard and Asa Kemp, January 5, 1841, JSP.

57. Overseer Contract between James Sheppard and Charles B. Crocker, July 12, 1844, JSP.

58. Overseer Contract between James Sheppard and Thomas Senoir, January 2, 1847, JSP.

59. Overseer Contract, July 15, 1851, between James Sheppard and D. T. Weeks, JSP; Records from Sulpher Springs Plantation, 1850–1851, JSP. This record shows that Weeks remitted the cost of 41 lbs. of meat to Sheppard in 1851. Overseer Contract between James Sheppard and D. T. Weeks, 1855, JSP; Overseer Contract between James Sheppard and D. T. Weeks, May 27, 1856, JSP.

60. Overseer Contract between James Sheppard and Robert W. Miller, February 7, 1859, JSP.
61. Overseer Contract between James Sheppard and J. M. Key, July 23, 1860, JSP; Overseer Contract between James Sheppard and William F. Black, April 9, 1960, JSP.
62. This was a standard practice. See, for example, Receipt for wages and deduction of items furnished to Charles B. Crocker, 1846, JSP; receipt for wages and deduction of items furnished to David T. Weeks, 1856, JSP; receipt for wages and deduction of items furnished to David T. Weeks, 1857, JSP.
63. Letter from David T. Weeks to James Sheppard, September 22, 1859, JSP.
64. Roberts v. Brownrigg, 9 Ala. 106, 108 (1846).
65. Cresap v. Winter, 14 La. 553, 553 (1840).
66. Ibid.
67. Ibid.
68. Ibid.
69. Ibid.
70. Ibid., p. 554.
71. Ibid., p. 554.
72. Ibid., pp. 553, 556.
73. Ibid., p. 556.
74. Garcia v. Garcia, 7 La. Ann. 525, 526 (1852).
75. Ibid., p. 526.
76. Ibid.
77. Ibid., p. 526.
78. Ibid., p. 527.
79. Ibid., p. 526.
80. Ibid., p. 527.
81. Ibid.
82. Ibid.
83. Lambert v. King, 12 La. Ann. 662 (1856). Even though Elodie Lambert was a woman who owned a plantation, she operated within the patriarchal strictures of plantation ownership and management. For more on how woman planters and enslavers navigated the plantation economy, see Stephanie E. Jones-Rogers, *They Were Her Property: White Woman as Slave Owners in the American South* (New Haven: Yale University Press, 2019); Wood, *Masterful Women*.
84. Lambert v. King, 12 La. Ann., 662.
85. Ibid.
86. Ibid.
87. Ibid.
88. Ibid.
89. Ibid.
90. Ibid., 663.
91. Pettigrew v. Bishop, 3 Ala. 440 (1842).

Chapter 3

"Pushing" Torture, Managing Violence, and Planter Regulation of Overseer Control

"PUSHING" TORTURE

The plantation as the vehicle to wealth was tied to the primacy of cotton in the growth of global capitalism. The large-scale cultivation and harvest of cotton required new forms of labor organization, as well as labor management. Enter the overseer. By 1860, there were approximately 38,000 overseers working as plantation managers throughout the antebellum south.[1] They were employed by the wealthiest of planters, planters who held multiple plantations and owned hundreds of enslaved Africans.[2] By 1860, 85 percent of all cotton grown in the South was on plantations of 100 acres or more.[3] On these plantations resided 91.2 percent of enslaved Africans.[4] Planters came to own these Africans through the internal slave trade in the United States that moved to its cotton fields approximately one million enslaved laborers.[5] Between 1800 and 1860, the amount of cotton enslaved Africans cultivated and picked increased from 1.4 million pounds to 2 billion pounds.[6] These enslaved persons picked cotton with such growing efficiency that by 1820 cotton comprised 42 percent of exports from the United States and accounted for the majority of all cotton traded worldwide.[7]

The bulk of the 38,000 overseers managed the one million enslaved on thousands of plantation acres. It was not Eli Whitney's cotton gin or higher quality cottonseed that led to the production of two billion pounds of U.S. cotton on the world market in 1860.[8] Rather, it was the evolution of the gang system of labor organization, the exploitation and torture of enslaved African labor, and the rise of plantation management schemes that translated both into plantation wealth.[9] Gang labor organization granted overseers the ability to surveil the workforce and monitor productivity.[10] Overseers walked or rode horses down rows of labor organized by rows of cotton. They forced productivity by the whip or by their menacing presence to urge the enslaved to keep up or suffer the consequences.[11] This process was part and parcel of what Edward Baptist has termed the "pushing system," or a system of forced labor productivity where the fastest enslaved set the pace of cotton picking for their row, and the overseer enforced that pace through whipping, maiming, and sometimes death for the enslaved who could not match or exceed the pace.[12] In his sweeping, comprehensive study of the global cotton economy, Baptist describes the pushing system through the eyes of an enslaved man, Charles Ball. He writes

> As Ball lined up by the first waist-high cotton plant of his row, he was about to learn a new way of working, one meant to occupy most of the waking moments remaining to him on earth. He saw Simon [another enslaved man] take a row, lift his hoe, and begin to work rapidly down the side of his furrow. Everyone else began to do the same in a great hurry. Ball could see that each of them had to chop all the weeds in their row without damaging the cotton plants. But then the man in the next row warned him that no one was allowed to fall behind the captain. Ball realized thus "the overseer had nothing to do but to keep Simon hard at work, and he was certain that all others must work equally hard." And the overseer was already stalking down the rows, whip in hand. Ball kept his head down and kept his hoe moving, trying to keep up with Simon's furious pace.[13]

Ball witnessed the consequences for failure to keep pace when on the day he began laboring on a new plantation, the overseer summoned him to witness as three women were whipped for laziness, failure to properly prepare their cotton after picking, and otherwise for dereliction of their duties.[14]

Historian Walter Johnson in *River of Dark Dreams: Slavery and Empire in the Cotton Kingdom* describes a range of punishments for falling behind the picking pace including:

> fifteen lashes; thirty lashes; two hundred; four hundred; so severely that the fibers of the shirt healed "fast to my back"; until "my clothes were all full of blood that flowed from my own body"; "until the blood ran out of his shoes"; so that he was out of work for ten days; two weeks, three weeks, five months; so that he "knew nothing for two days"; so that it was five weeks before he could walk; so that "he was always subject to fits after that"; so that "no pen can ever describe what my feelings were"; so that language itself collapsed under the onslaught.[15]

Johnson eloquently notes that "these were the standard measures of cotton production, measuring the speed and efficiency of the process by which capital and labor were transformed into cotton."[16] So integral was torture to the plantation economy that as early as 1834 E. Thomas published *A Concise View of the Slavery of the People of Colour in the United States: Exhibiting Some of the Most Affecting Cases of Cruel and Barbarous Treatment of the Slaves by Their Most Inhuman and Brutal Masters Not Heretofore Published: And also Showing Absolute Necessity for the Most Speedy Abolition of Slavery, with an Endeavor to Point Out the Best Means of Effecting It*.[17] Forms of torture noted in the table of contents for the book include: "The infant whipped to death with a cow-skin; The aged woman starved to death; The man that had his teeth knocked out; the rash overseer; The slave shot by her master; The slave slowly dissected and burnt; The man and wife yoked like oxen; [and] The pregnant woman whipped."[18] At the time Thomas published his book, he believed his examples to be among the worst treatment of slaves. Accordingly, he declined to "name names" to save the planters and their overseers from embarrassment for their actions.[19] The ubiquitous recounting of torture and cotton production speaks to a contrary reality. Unfathomable forms of brutality were the rule and not the exception. Solomon Northup provides an illuminating summary of the overseer's role in maintaining the constant threat of violence required to sustain the slave regime. He writes:

> On larger estates, employing fifty or a hundred, or perhaps two hundred hands, an overseer is deemed indispensable. These gentlemen ride into the field on horseback, without an exception, to my knowledge, armed with pistols, bowie knife, whip, and accompanied by several dogs. They follow, equipped in this fashion, in the rear of the slaves, keeping a sharp look-out upon them all. The requisite qualifications in an overseer are utter heartlessness, brutality, and cruelty. It is his business to produce large crops, and if that is accomplished, no matter what amount of human suffering it may have cost. The presence of dogs are necessary to overhaul a fugitive who may take to his heels, as is sometimes the case, when faint or sick, he is unable to maintain his row, and unable also, to endure the whip. The pistols reserved for any dangerous emergency, there having been instances when such weapons were necessary. Goaded into uncontrollable madness, even the slave will sometimes turn upon his oppressor. The gallows were standing at Marksville last January upon which one was executed a year ago for killing his overseer.[20]

Between 1805 and 1855, the pushing system and its accoutrements of torture altered planter expectations for how many acres enslaved hands could cultivate from 5 acres to 10.[21] These expectations were memorialized in the field of plantation management.

Chapter 3

MANAGING VIOLENCE

The discipline of modern management began in the cotton fields of the antebellum south.[22] The growing scale of plantation land, the enslaved labor force working the land, and their increasing value precipitated the emergence of a managerial class of workers—overseers.[23] Overseers marked the divides between ownership, authority, and control over land and the enslaved. As managers, they were regarded as implementing the minds of their planter employers, owners of the enslaved, through their authority and control over the bodies of the enslaved. This is in sharp contrast to the slave drivers, enslaved individuals tasked with implementing the will of the overseer over the bodies of his fellow enslaved.[24] As journalist Frederick Law Olmsted observed in his work *The Cotton Kingdom*,

> [the cruelty of slavery] was emphasized by a tall and powerful negro who walked to and fro in the rear of the line, frequently cracking his whip, and calling out in the surliest manner, to one and another, "Shove your hoe, there! shove your hoe!" .... The whip was evidently in constant use .... There were no rules on the subject that I learned; the overseers and drivers punished the negroes whenever they deemed it necessary and in such manner, and with such severity, as they thought fit."[25]

Olmstead also recalled hearing from overseers " 'If you don't work faster,' or 'If you don't work better,' or 'If you don't recollect what I tell you, I will have you flogged.' "[26] When he asked the overseer whether he found the constant punishment he meted out on the enslaved to be distasteful, the overseer replied " 'Yes, it would be to those who are not used to it—it's my business and I think nothing of it. Why sir, I wouldn't mind killing a nigger more that I would a dog [but I have] not quite [done] that.' "[27] Specific terms in overseer contracts served to further circumscribe drivers's authority and subject them to overseer will.[28] White supremacy and patriarchy were the entry points considered for competent management. With those threshold characteristics satisfied, however, only those White men with enough literacy and numeracy to meet the demands of plantation management record-keeping and the mettle for violence could hope to be hired as overseers. Capitalism sorted White men in the plantation economy by whether their labor was in direct competition with the enslaved or in support of planters' acquisition and maintenance of land and the enslaved—potential competition with planters outside of the planter class was neither desirable nor marketable.[29] White men able to support and facilitate planter wealth accumulation comprised the pool of potential overseers whose management expectations and limits for labor productivity were made clear in a complex system of public law, management tools, and private contract.

Legislators sanitized statutory provisions governing the treatment of the enslaved to prohibit violence and to require that they be treated with some measure of humanity.[30] Numerous pieces of legislation enacted by the Mississippi, Georgia, and Alabama legislatures are illustrative. The 1848 Alabama Slave Code made it "the duty of every master, or other person having charge of Slaves, to treat them with humanity, and provide for them necessary food and clothing."[31] If a slave owner was indicted under this provision, then at trial, the jury would decide the meaning of "necessary food and clothing."[32] Once found guilty, an enslaver could face a fine of $25 to $1,000.[33] By 1852, the Alabama Legislature had modified this statute to state with specificity the roles of planters, enslaved labor, and their managers under the plantation regime. The updated Slave Code states in relevant part:

> §2042 The state or condition of negro or African slavery is established by law in this state; conferring on the master property in and the right to the time, labor and services of the slave, and to enforce obedience on the part of the slave, to all his lawful commands. This authority he may delegate to another.
>
> §2043 The master must treat his slave with humanity, and must not inflict upon him any cruel punishment; he must provide him with a sufficiency of healthy food and necessary clothing; cause him to be properly attended during sickness, and provide for his necessary wants in old age.[34]

Unlike earlier provisions, these provisions acknowledge the transferable nature of a (slave)master/planter's control over an enslaved's time, will, and labor to an overseer. But regardless of a planter's ability to transfer his managerial authority over his enslaved to an overseer, his duty to them remained with him alone. The Mississippi Legislature made this distinction plain in a similar statute:

> It shall be the duty of owners of slaves to treat them with humanity, to provide for them the necessary clothing and provisions, and to abstain from injuries to them extending to endanger life or limb; and if any owner, hirer, or employer of slaves shall have failed to supply them necessary clothing and provisions, or shall have treated them with inhumanity, the person so offending may be indicted therefor, and on conviction shall be fined in any sum not exceeding five hundred dollars, or may be imprisoned in the country jail not exceeding three months, or both, at the discretion of the court.[35]

Again, the beginning of the statute sets out the duties of planter/enslavers only, no other group, with respect to the enslaved, while the latter portion discusses dereliction of duty by planter/enslavers and breaches of authority delegated to other White men (hirers or employers of enslaved persons) as they aided the planter in upholding his duties. This distinction is significant, because as these statutes make clear, planters (slave owners) had both property and labor rights in the bodies of the enslaved, among which they could decide what to transfer to overseers. With that transfer, the overseer gained a legal obligation by statute to safeguard the property—enslaved labor—owned by the planter. These statutory obligations were memorialized in the private employment contracts between planters and overseers. It is through such contracts that planters maintained the fiction of paternalism, their role as dutiful fathers benevolently caring for their enslaved, while transferring authority and responsibility for navigating the realities of daily plantation life to overseers.[36] Planters were able to perpetuate the myth of paternalism, because overseers took on statutory and contractual obligations that allowed them to be punished for the maltreatment of the enslaved. The twin themes of duty and transferable authority present in these statutory provisions continued as legislatures passed laws governing the punishment of the enslaved, and overseers sued planters over alleged contractual breaches for their inability to competently do the same.

The Mississippi legislature placed checks on violence toward the enslaved by making "cruel or unusual punishment" by masters and those under their authority subject to a fine of up to $500, or twelve months of imprisonment in the county jail at the court's discretion, or both.[37] A similar Georgia law elaborated on what constituted cruel and unusual punishment by enumerating "unnecessary or excessive whipping . . . withholding proper food and sustenance . . . requiring greater labor from such slave or slaves than he, she, or they are able to perform [and] not affording proper clothing."[38] The Georgia legislature further elucidated that overseers were a class of White men to whom planter authority over enslaved labor could be delegated by providing criminal penalties for "any person *except* the owner, overseer, or employer of a slave, who shall beat, whip, or wound such slave."[39] In the stratified labor structure of the plantation economy, White men's status vis-à-vis the enslaved was held superior. His right to the bodies of the enslaved and their labor was quite another matter.

In its 1852 Slave Code, the Alabama Legislature set forth the penalty for treating the enslaved with inhumanity and cruelty. It provided that "[any] master, or other person standing toward the slave in that relation, who inflicts, or allows another to inflict on him" cruel or inhumane treatment including withholding sufficient food, clothing, care when sick, and maintenance in old age could be fined between $25 and $1,000.[40] Subsequent statutes that governed indictments and trials under this provision required that the juries in those trials comprise two-thirds slaveholders.[41] This requirement all but guaranteed that any slaveholders tried for inhumanity and cruelty would be looked upon favorably by slaveholders (planters), who could be held to the same standard if similarly accused. Likewise, any overseers tried under the same statute would have a group of racial peers with an interest in preserving their social status as paternal caretakers, as well as their wealth, which was largely dependent on overseer violence in managing their enslaved. This struggle over the limits of overseer authority in managing enslaved labor played out in civil cases concerning breach of contract and criminal cases involving the deaths of the enslaved.

In 1856, the Arkansas Supreme Court adjudicated a case brought by an overseer against a planter for nonpayment of wages owed under an overseer contract from 1853.[42] The overseer, Martin, sued a planter, Brunson, for unpaid wages for services rendered in 1853.[43] Martin was employed from March 1, 1853, to October 15, 1853.[44] His employment ended when he killed Nathan, an enslaved under his supervision.[45] Martin argued that his services for that seven-month period were worth between $250 and $450, and introduced his contract with Brunson to verify he agreed to oversee Brunson's plantations for the sum of $250 in 1853.[46] By all accounts, the crop for 1853 was passable, even though the yield was not as high as other plantations in the area.[47]

Brunson claimed that he was entitled to damages for Nathan's death—Nathan was valued from $1,200 to $1,500 at time he was killed—which is why Brunson had not paid Martin's wages.[48] The court reasoned that the planter could offset the damage amount for any wages owed, provided the enslaved died as a result of the overseers mismanagement.[49] Because Nathan's worth was in excess of the amount Brunson owed Martin for his services as overseer, Brunson sought to collect the difference from Martin as an offset amount.

At trial, evidence was given that Brunson's enslaved were difficult to manage and hard-pressed to work in the absence of an overseer—actions for which they allegedly had been whipped by the overseer employed in 1852.[50] Just prior to Nathan's death, Martin remarked in a conversation at a store near the Brunson plantation that he "had a rough and saucy set of hands to manage, and that, after that, if he ever overseed [sic] again, he would make the negroes obey him, or he would kill them."[51] Witnesses to the conversation said that Martin was drinking, but calm, in good spirits, and not drunk.[52] Shortly after he left the store, Martin went back to the cotton plantation carrying his whip.[53] There he encountered Nathan and told him that he, Martin, had "come for [Nathan's] shirt."[54] Because Martin approached Nathan with his whip, Martin's directive for Nathan to take off his shirt was likely so that Martin could whip him. Nathan told Martin that he had taken off his shirt for the last overseer, to which Martin replied, upon drawing his gun on Nathan, that he "had come for his shirt, and intended to have it or hurt him."[55] Nathan responded, "shoot or be damned," and Martin obliged, shooting him at least three times until he was dead.⁵⁶ At the time of his death, Nathan held no weapons, but only cotton in one hand.⁵⁷ Martin claimed that Nathan came toward him once his drew his gun, as if to knock it away, but medical evidence introduced at trial contradicted this claim.⁵⁸ Evidence was also introduced that Nathan was "a stout negro, weighing about 200 pounds with bodily strength enough to crush [Martin] down."⁵⁹ Martin was described as "a cripple."⁶⁰

Upon submitting the case to the jury, the judge gave it three instructions, among them: "1st. That to enable [Brunson] to [recover damages for Nathan's death], it must appear to the jury that [Nathan's death] was the result of [Martin's] mismanagement as [Brunson's overseer]; 2d. [*sic*] In order to allow [Brunson] to [recover damages for Nathan's death], it must appear from the testimony, that [Martin] negligently and without necessity, killed [Nathan]."⁶¹ The jury found in favor of Martin, allowing him to recover his wages under the 1853 contract.⁶² By their verdict they deemed Martin an adequate overseer and Nathan's death a legally justifiable loss in Martin's management of the Brunson plantation. Of note is that this is one of the first breach of contract cases tried in Arkansas where the overseer was not required to be tried for murder and convicted prior to the planter recovering monetary damages for the death of an enslaved.⁶³ This law was changed by Arkansas statute. The relevant provision provides that "in no case shall the right of action of any party injured in the commission of a felony, be deemed adjudged to be merged in such felony; but damages sustained thereby may be recovered in action brought for that purpose."⁶⁴

The Alabama Supreme Court also grappled with the limits of overseer authority to punish the enslaved for committing criminal offenses.⁶⁵ While under contract, an overseer, Senter "violently [beat], [bruised] and [ill-treated] a negro man named Hamilton, [who belonged to Gillian]."⁶⁶ Gillian subsequently sued Senter for trespass, inflicting harm upon the body of his property (Hamilton), on grounds that Senter's authority did not extend to punish Hamilton for criminal offenses.⁶⁷ At the time he was whipped, Hamilton was accused of stealing from one of Gillian's neighbors, L. D. Griffith.⁶⁸ Griffith told Senter that he would drop any charges against Hamilton for theft if Senter beat him.⁶⁹ The jury found Senter guilty after being instructed that an overseer's authority did not extend to punishing slaves for criminal offenses, which rested in the power of the state.⁷⁰ In an unusually long exposition on overseer authority, the court wrote:

> The overseer of slaves, under a contract with the master, to supervise and direct their operations must be considered to some extent as standing in *loco magisteri* [in the place of the master]; and of necessity invested with authority to inflict reasonable punishment for the breach of police regulations. *What are, or should*

be, the disciplinary rules upon a plantation, it is very difficult to define, yet there are some points in respect to the government of slaves, in which perhaps all of us are agreed. It is certainly for the interest of the master, that the slave should be taught habits of industry; and as a moral, sentient being, should learn that his happiness depends upon the appreciation of virtue, and a conformity to its precepts. If these sentiments cannot be inculcated by the force of moral suasion, it is certainly allowable, and it may be a duty to inflict corporal punishment.[71]

Although it was commonly understood to be the responsibility of the master/planter, and in his absence the overseer, to instill morality and industry in the enslaved by subjecting them to punishment and torture, the ultimate duty to protect the enslaved rested with the paternal planter, the plantation father; breaches of this authority transferred to overseers was actionable only when they abused this authority.[72] Six years later, the Alabama legislature would codify this duty in its 1852 Slave Code.[73] By and large courts condoned a wide range of punishments leading to injury and death, for this was the unknowable, "difficult to define" disciplinary realm of the plantation. Beating an enslaved pregnant woman to miscarriage[74] or shooting an enslaved man described as "ungovernable"[75] did not warrant overseer payment to their owners beyond medical costs when applicable. When the estate of a deceased planter, Mr. Johnson, sued an overseer, Mr. Lovett, for whipping an enslaved woman, Dinah, with a cowhide, kicking her in the stomach, and knocking out her tooth, no damages were assessed against Lovett beyond Dinah's medical bills.[76] The Georgia Supreme Court did find that had Mr. Johnson suffered any damages as a result of Dinah's beating, Lovett would have been liable for them because his conduct was "unbecoming" an overseer.[77] However, Dinah's doctor observed her "going about as sprightly as ever" after her recovery, and the court noted that her lost tooth was not likely to diminish her market value.[78] Courts sanctioned the everyday violence of plantation management, necessary for cotton production and the continuance of the global plantation economy. Civil lawsuits to recover damages for injury to or the deaths of the enslaved were decided in favor of overseers, as long as their punishment of the enslaved was not in excess of punishments common on plantations.[79] To quote the Louisiana Supreme Court on the matter:

[the] master "may correct and chastise [the enslaved], though not with unusual rigor, nor so as to maim or mutilate him, or to expose him to danger of loss of life, or to cause his death" . . . the planter who employs an overseer in absence of orders to the contrary, delegates to him the power of punishment contemplated by law, and necessary for the preservation of discipline and the public peace. But certainly, the overseer is restricted by the same measure of power which the

law has imposed upon the owner; and, if he transgresses it, he violates his duty, and is answerable to his employer in damages, and to public justice, which he has offended.[80]

Ironically courts maintained the fiction, through its adjudication of these matters, that punishment and torture of enslaved men and women were somehow separate from an overseer's ability to "make a good crop." In two separate instances, the Louisiana Supreme Court pointed out that even though overseers had treated slaves cruelly and punished them excessively they had managed their respective plantations adequately. Of overseer Hendricks in *Hendricks v. Phillips*, the court stated that he "was an attentive overseer and made a good crop for his employer [Phillips]."[81] In *Dwyer v. Cane*, the court explained that overseer Dwyer made a good cotton crop for Cain, his planter employer, "but evidence in the record, which the [trial court] judge appeared to have believed, shows, that he inflicted cruel and unusual punishments upon the male slaves, and that his conduct with the women of the plantation was grossly and openly immoral."[82] It concluded its judgment by stating definitively "[cruelty] to slaves is a sufficient cause of dismissal, and *honeste viviere* [honorable and virtuous living] forms part of the duties of an overseer."[83] The Mississippi Supreme Court followed suit in *Prichard v. Martin*, finding that despite overseer Martin's maltreatment of the enslaved and possibly disrespect to his planter employer (Prichard), there was no evidence that he was derelict in his duties as an overseer.[84] According to witness testimony at trial, Prichard had remarked that "Martin was a good overseer, and that [Prichard] was much pleased with him; that he had been informed, before employing him, that [Martin] was a cruel man, but that [Martin] has been misrepresented, and was not as cruel as [Prichard][who] had been in the habit of frequently turning off his overseers."[85]

Slave deaths tried as criminal offenses enforced the same boundaries of overseer punishment, and resulted only in criminal sanctions for cruel and unusual punishment. For example in *Jordan v. State*, Randall Jordan, the overseer, was indicted for murdering an enslaved girl Mariah, who was owned by John Dawson.[86] Medical evidence was introduced at trial to show that Jordan whipped Mariah to death by "blows inflicted on her back, thighs, and belly [with bruises] all over. . . down to her muscles."[87] The blood from the wounds had clotted in some places on her body, which was proof of a prolonged beating.[88] Another witness, Captain N. R. Roberts, testified that Mariah "seemed to have been cut to the bone on the thigh, and the wounds were filled and clotted with blood."[89] He also observed that Mariah appeared to be thirteen years of age, and that the strap Jordan used to beat her was too thick and therefore inappropriate for use on someone her size.[90] Roberts noted that a switch would have been more appropriate.[91] Additionally, Jordan hit

Mariah's father, Spencer, when he tried to help her during Jordan's beating.[92] In the court's words, "[Mariah] was then lying dead or dying, and the prisoner's refusal to allow her father to go to her aid and relief under these circumstances, was certainly evidence of deeply seated malice against the girl he had beaten."[93] It went on to state that "[Jordan] had power over [Mariah]." He exercised it most cruelly, inflicting on her a beating, from 400 to over 1,000 blows, which showed in the language of the law "an abandoned and maligned heart."[94] The trial court convicted Jordan of manslaughter, his sentence set at the court's discretion.[95] Jordan appealed, but the Supreme Court of Georgia upheld his conviction.[96]

Likewise, in *State v. Flanigin*, an overseer, Flanigin, was convicted of killing an enslaved man, Jacob.[97] Flanigin struck Jacob repeatedly in the head with a whip handle, causing his death.[98] The medical examiner testified that Flanigin administered "many blows and stripes . . . with great violence; all of which together [were] sufficient to cause his death."[99] Flanigin was convicted of murder in the second degree and imprisoned to ten years in the penitentiary.[100] He appealed and the Supreme Court of Alabama upheld his conviction.[101]

The stakes for mismanagement under criminal prosecution included a call to account outside of the realm of private contract, a kingdom tightly controlled by White men with a personal interest in the plantation economy. In the criminal courts, overseers convicted for killing enslaved men and women were called to public justice by relinquishing their freedom, an all but iron-clad right of White manhood. Cases like Jordan and Flanigin's, where appellate courts upheld overseer convictions for murdering the enslaved, were rare. It comes as no surprise that even in cases where trial juries voted to convict overseers for killing the enslaved in their charge, appellate courts often reversed those convictions to reinstate that right.[102]

PLANTER REGULATION OF OVERSEER CONTROL

Southern legislatures also enacted legislation that subjected the bodies of enslaved Africans to seemingly unceasing surveillance, to ensure their subordination to the planters who owned them and the overseers who managed them.[103] For example, statutes in Alabama and Mississippi prohibited the enslaved from hiring themselves out;[104] being in spaces at planter or overseer houses for more than a specified number of hours and without planter or overseer permission;[105] gathering in groups on plantations other than their own except to attend church services, funerals, or otherwise permitted by planters and overseers;[106] and leaving their plantations without a pass.[107] The authority to surveil was transferred to overseers by law, and planters were prosecuted for noncompliance. Consider, for example, the case of Alabaman planter William P. Molett.[108] Molett owned a piece of land large enough to accommodate his family home, five Alabaman plantations, and living quarters for his enslaved laborers.[109] On this land, called Mill Place, Molett employed no overseer to manage his enslaved laborers, but insisted that "he acted as overseer of his own slaves, and was a vigilant overseer."[110] Molett alleged that he was often on site at Mill Place tending to his enslaved labor.[111] He further alleged that he did not leave the property for more than week-long intervals, but did leave each day to return to his home located four miles away.[112] Unconvinced, the State of Alabama indicted him for violating its statute that required an owner or overseer to reside on plantations with an enslaved labor force of more than six.[113] Although the Alabama Supreme Court reversed his conviction and remanded the case on a procedural technicality, it emphasized that the law was within the state's police power granted to it by the United States Constitution to "[prevent] crime, [preserve] peace, and good order, and [secure] life and property."[114] As the Alabama legislature made clear, the state's exercise of this particular policing regulation was to help the White men of its state to "more effectually secure subordination among slaves, by requiring the owner, or overseer to reside with them."[115] This authority was also reflected in the language of overseer's employment contracts with planters and in the expectations by plantation management manuals.[116]

It is difficult to ascertain when Vincent A. Peirson began his work as overseer at the Cookshay Plantation in Chambers County, Alabama. However, he appears as a salaried employee of the Jackson family as early as 1842.[117] While no contract marks his commencement of overseer duties in that year, a contract survives for 1847 between himself, Martha J. Jackson, and her son Henry R. Jackson. The contract is a lengthy document that outlines in detail Mr. Peirson's obligations as overseer at Cookshay. It places in his care twenty-five adult field hands, seventeen youth, and four old enslaved laborers, for a total of forty-six persons.[118] According to the document, Peirson agreed to enter into the job of overseer under the following terms:

> He [Peirson] engages to pay the most *unremitting* attention to every kind of plantation stock, and to have the best care taken of every kind of plantation tools and instrument. He is also to give his personal attention to the daily work of the hands entrusted to his charge, *never leaving them*, except when called away by business connected with the plantation, or from occasions which appear perfectly satisfactory to his own sense of duty . . . . He will continue the most humane treatment of the Negroes, *having every needful attention paid them in all cases of sickness* . . . .[119]

Similar terms appear in an overseer contract between overseer William Whitley and planter John Murray. Whitley agreed to work as an overseer on Murray's plantation in Lowndes County, Alabama, on terms that he is never to leave or absent himself from said plantation on business at any time during [Murray's] absence from the state, and only with [Murray's] consent when [he is] on the plantation; he is never to drink ardent spirits to intoxication, while in [Murray's] employ; he is not to maltreat any of [Murray's] slaves, and is to give his personal attention to [Murray's] business; and failing to comply fully with all or either of these conditions or stipulations, the said Whitley is to leave [Murray's] employment, at [his] discretion, without the least remuneration for the time he may have served [Murray].[120]

For his one-year term of employment from January of 1858–1859, Whitley would receive $400 salary paid in cash along with various food items.[121] Two months into the contract, Whitley, it seems, had enough.[122] In a scathing letter to Murray, Whitley wrote, "I will not stay any longer than this letter has time to give you word, and for you to come or send out; I will relieve you the trouble of discharging me on the spot."[123] Whitley sued Murray for the prorated salary amount up to the time of his departure. For his impudence and breach of contract terms, he received no wages.[124]

As both Pierson's and Whitley's contracts make clear, planters and overseers incurred different burdens for ownership and management of plantation land and the enslaved men, women, and children who worked it. To planters went the duty to care for their land and labor; to overseers went the obligations inherent in their transferred authority to do so. Demands on overseer time comprised a large portion of those obligations, and served as a check on their freedom as White men to allocate their labor as they pleased to anyone other than the planter. As Thomas Affleck admonished in *The Duties of an Overseer*:

[Bear] in mind that a fine crop consists, first, in an increase in the number, and marked improvement in the condition and value of negroes; second, and abundance of provision of all sorts for man and beast, carefully saved and properly housed; . . . fourth, an improvement in the productive qualities of the land, and in the general condition of the plantation . . . then—as heavy a crop of cotton, sugar, or rice, as could possibly be made under the circumstances, sent to market in good season and of prime quality.[125]

While public law, contracts, and litigation subjected African bodies to almost constant surveillance by White men, overseers subjected themselves to the same by taking contractual responsibility for the planter's economic return.

In addition to contract provisions that integrated such directives, manuals developed for plantation management further solidified the relationship between duty and authority, ownership and control. Affleck reminded overseers that they had undertaken the responsibility to act upon every command given by their employer in the best way possible. He opined that such a responsibility required "more than [the overseer's] mere presence on the plantation, and that, at such times as suits your own pleasure and convenience."[126] Quoting George Washington's "Instructions to his Overseers," instructions that Affleck had no doubt adopted as his own, he urged overseers to remain at home unless summoned by inescapable business or worship because slaves were unlikely to work hard or at all in the overseer's absence.[127] Shirking of duties, according to Washington's instructions and Affleck's agreement, was more severe than stealing his (Washington's) money.[128] It was "a breach of trust," one that released the planter from carrying out his duties outlined in the employment agreement.[129]

Civil and criminal litigation concerning overseer breaches of conduct underscored that the submission and productivity of enslaved laborers were the dual aims of plantation management. "Never be induced by a course of good behavior on the part of negroes, to relax the strictness of your discipline," cautioned Affleck.[130] He went on, "but, when you have by judicious management, brought them to that state, keep them so by the same means."[131] Overseers, it would seem from litigation over their conduct alone, were prone to intemperance, brutishness, and excess in their management of the enslaved. They needed the structure of plantation management to enact discipline on the planter's land and labor, and, in turn, to be disciplined by its tenets themselves. The memorialization of these patriarchal and capitalist boundaries in formal managerial instructions was an extension of overseer obligations imposed by contract and statute. They proved burdensome to overseers as they worked to document plantation productivity and establish themselves as competent managers. Although adherence to the tenets of plantation management provided planters with the badge of innovator, it also placed greater responsibilities and time commitments upon overseers. Like contract provisions and common practices that required overseers to devote the majority of their time attending to plantation business, plantation management was yet another factor that set clear boundaries for overseer upward mobility. Attendance to planter needs left overseers without the time to attend to their own pursuits, or the inclination to form an image of themselves as managers outside of planter control

The Cotton Plantation Record and Account Book, No.1 Suitable for a Force of 40 Hands, or Under, by Thomas Affleck, was a popular organizing tool for followers of plantation management.[132] First published in 1847 and in its fifth edition in 1857, the book contained pre-printed pages structured like charts and diaries for the overseer to enter every possible daily occurrence on the plantation.[133] As the page marked Explanation and Record of Accounts states in part:

> The pages marked A, constitute the daily record of all that transpires upon the plantation, worthy of being recorded-such as the kind of work being done, and

the number of hands engaged in it; when plowing planting, sowing, scraping, etc. began; when the first forms, blossoms, and open bolls appeared; the state of the weather and forwardness of the crops; the first appearance and continued progress of the caterpillar and of other insects which injure the crops, with every fact of importance relative to them; the behavior, good or bad, of the negroes; and every other item which may be of value for future reference.

. . . It is important that the entries be made on the evening of each day. If persevered in, such a duty becomes a habit.[134]

Following this lengthy account were further explanations of the purposes for which each specially marked page was to be used. Pages marked "B" were for property inventories; "C" for the amount of cotton picked weekly; "D" for items given to slaves; "E" for keeping record of all supplies; "F" for lists of slave deaths and births; "G" for checking physicians accounts; "H" for weight of cotton for sale; "I" for the valuation of slaves; "J" for stock inventory; "K" for tool inventory; "L" for products of the plantation; "M" for the yearly cotton sales;. "N" for plantation expenses; and "O" for listings of credits, debits, and expenses.[135] Overseers used the pages of Affleck's manual to document enslaved productivity as a reflection of their management acumen. However, even in accounting, the roles of planter and overseer mirrored duty and authority. Planters had the privilege of ownership and the duty of taxation, and usually filled in forms that correlated to their position as owners.[136] Overseers had the authority to compel labor to a level of productivity that proved that value.[137] Their accounting practices similarly reflected the authority transferred to them.

To facilitate overseers' accounting, it was common for enslaved men, women, and children to be classified according to the amount of labor they could lend to the cultivation of the crop. The term "hand" to describe enslaved labor did not refer merely to their actual hands, but rather to the wealth potential of those hands in making a good crop.[138] Explained so expressively by Edward E. Baptist in *The Half Has Never Been Told*,

> [the] word [hand] delivered because it was continually recalculated from a thousand different economic relations. As he was buying enslaved people, the white man, in his mind's eye, saw himself working them, reselling them, mortgaging them, making them into money, putting them "in his pocket" . . . sellers, auctioneers, buyers, and bidders did specific things to make whole people look and in certain ways to be like the obedient right hands enslavers' future endeavors.[139]

At the top of the heap were "prime field hands," a group comprised of "enslaved [men] or [women] whose productivity was among the maximum that could be expected from a single individual."[140] Generally, a prime field hand's value was "ten thousand times the price of cotton, i.e. if cotton were at ten cents per pound, the [enslaved] would cost $1,000."[141] All other enslaved labor was valued based on gradations from a prime field hand's value. The elderly, breast-feeding, and otherwise infirm were known as the "trash gang" of laborers and considered "half-hands."[142] Children more than ten years old were "quarter hands."[143] These classifications allowed enslaved labor to be commoditized, sorted, and compared yearly on the same plantation, thus measuring effective (or ineffective) overseer management. The amounts of cotton picked set the average by classification of hands, and also set the pace of pushing and punishment.[144] Tables 3.1–3.3 show the amount and value of labor for the enslaved women, girls, men, and boys for one week's work on Joseph M. Jaynes' Plantation in Mississippi.[145]

These records reflect the amount of cotton in pounds and value, the staggering amounts of labor for which enslaved men and women were forced to sacrifice their bodies to the gods of capitalism and cotton. Even regulated by statute and management manual was how the enslaved utilized the Sabbath. The Alabama, Arkansas, and Georgia legislatures passed laws prohibiting anyone from allowing the enslaved to work on Sunday.[146] Far from a benign, beneficent gesture, Affleck's instructions to overseers on Sabbath observance provide a more ominous context for these laws—the ongoing system of punishments and rewards that would make an overseer's authority more (or less) effective. He wrote:

> [When] it can be done without too great loss of time, the stocks offer a means of punishment greatly to be preferred—So secured in a lonely, quiet place, where no communication can be held with any one, nothing but bread and water allowed, and the confinement extending from Saturday when they drop work, until Sabbath evening, will prove much more effectual in preventing a repetition of the offence, than any amount of whipping.[147]

The Sabbath was an important tool by which to exact greater control over enslaved labor. In Affleck's words,

> [You] will find that an hour devoted every Sabbath morning to their moral and religious Instruction, would prove a great aid to you in bringing about a better state of things amongst the negroes. It has been thoroughly tried, and with the most satisfactory results, in many parts of the south. As a mere matter of interest, it has proved to be advisable—to say nothing of it as a point of duty. The effect upon their general good behavior, their cleanliness and good conduct on the Sabbath, is such as alone to recommend it to the Planter and Overseer.[148]

Keeping with the sorting and accounting practices for the enslaved and their labor, statutes required that they be valued for taxation according to the skills they added to the productivity of the crop. Affleck's form "I" facilitated

Table 3.1 Record of Cotton Picked on the Joseph M. Jaynes Plantation (MS) at Spring Field for the week of November 22, 1857 (Monday–Saturday)

Name	Sex	Age	Total Amt. of Cotton in lbs.
Amon (driver)	M	28	798
John	M	28	1,006[1]
Big George	M	31	727
Little George	M	22	762
Jim	M	27	90[2]
Edmond	M	35	768
Hampton	M	20	302[3]
Adam	M	18	1,133
Daniel	M	18	763
Frederic	M	27	729
Edward	M	15	625
Albert	M	12	409
Violet	F	24	995
Tempe	F	33	954
Caroline	F	17	820
Martha	F	24	820
Pharaby	F	22	897
Minden	F	45	308
Cely[4]	F	32	0[5]
Ester	F	14	597
Harriet	F	11	420
Sarah Ann	F	10	304
Little Eliza	F	16	158[6]
Ella	F	8	293

Source: The Cotton Plantation Record and Account Book, No. 1, "C."

[1] Daily Record of Cotton Picked on Joseph M. Jaynes Plantation, during the week commencing on November 22, 1857, JMJPJ. John picked cotton five days out of six this week. On Monday he was tasked with covering potatoes and tending to the cow pens.
[2] Ibid. Jim picked cotton one day this week. For the other five, he was tasked with driving the carriage.
[3] Ibid. Hampton picked cotton four days out of six this week. On Monday and Tuesday, he was tasked along with John to tend the cow pens and cover potatoes.
[4] There are two Celys listed on the enslaved valuation record for 1857 (one age thirty-two; the other age nine), but only one Cely listed on the record documenting the amount of cotton picked for the week of November 22, 1857. Given Cely's age and where she is listed in the weekly labor records, it is probable that the Cely whose labor is documented is the Cely who is thirty-two, not nine. Additionally, nine-year-old Cely is valued similarly to the girls in her seven- to ten-year-old age group. The Planter's Annual Record of his Negroes upon the Plantation, made at the commencement and at the close of the year 1857, JMJPJ; Daily Record of Cotton Picked on Joseph M. Jaynes Plantation, during the week commencing on November 22, 1857, JMJPJ.
[5] Cely is noted as "sick" for the week of November 22, 1857. Daily Record of Cotton Picked on Joseph M. Jaynes Plantation, during the week commencing on November 22, 1857, JMJPJ.
[6] Ibid. Monday–Wednesday, Little Eliza was at the plantation house.

planter documentation of enslaved persons' assessed value. The 1848 Alabama Slave Code provisions governing tax assessments is instructive. Assessors valued enslaved persons considered of high value ("mechanics, cooks, seamstresses, and barbers, or of some other trade, craft or occupation"), as well as those proven "unsound" or disabled when compared to their peers, at their discretion.[149] All other enslaved labor was valued as indicated

Table 3.2 Comparison Record of Cotton Picked on the Joseph M. Jaynes Plantation (MS) at Spring Field—Yield to Date (November 22, 1857)

Amount of cotton picked in lbs. for the week of November 22, 1857	14, 678
Amount of cotton picked in lbs. in the Spring Field prior to the week of November 22, 1857	69, 648
Total amount of cotton picked in lbs. in the Spring Field as of November 22, 1857	84,326
Estimated value in dollars in 1857 according to cotton price per pound	$10, 119.12
Estimated value in dollars in 2020 according to cotton price per pound	$300,218.01

Source: The Cotton Plantation Record and Account Book, No. 1, "C."

in table 3.4.[150] Statutory taxation provisions advised that real and personal property was to be assessed at its actual value, absent market speculation.[151] Tax returns from the Jackson plantation in Georgia suggest that the valuation practices codified in the Alabama statute were common in other southern states.[152] Table 3.5 documents the interplay between the assessed value of the enslaved for taxation purposes and the monetary value of their labor on the Joseph M. Jaynes Plantation.[153] Although tables 3.4 and 3.5 illustrate data from two different states, they show that enslaved labor in the age group considered "prime field hands" and valued most highly in table 3.5 were assessed for taxation in the Slave Code at a higher rate than non-skilled enslaved labor.

All of these carefully planned pages were provided to ensure that planters received an optimum return on their crops. As table 3.5 shows, if an enslaved person worked three or more days in a week, she/he exceeded the amount of labor needed per week to meet their assessed value.

Joseph M. Jaynes' use of Affleck's manual on his plantation in Rankin County, Mississippi, demonstrates how closely his overseers watched the work patterns of their enslaved charges to create a maximum return on Jayne's investment. Each of his overseers employed from 1854 to 1860 gave a detailed account of daily plantation life complete with cross-references to other years to show crop and enslaved labor progress, decline, or consistency. In several daily entries, Levy Alliston, overseer for Jaynes from 1854 to 1855, reported when the cotton planting was done, when the hands finished working the corn, when the cotton bloomed in 1855, and how those dates compared to when these tasks were undertaken and occurred during 1852–1854.[154] Other daily accounts illustrate the all-encompassing nature of plantation management for both overseers and the enslaved. For example, Alliston wrote on Wednesday (February 8, 1854) and Thursday (February 9, 1854) two entries that are typical of the specificity of Jaynes' account book. In his words:

Table 3.3 Estimated Value of Cotton Picked on the Joseph M. Jaynes Plantation (MS) in Spring Field for the Week of November 22, 1857, Per Enslaved Person

Name	Total Amount of Cotton Picked for the Week in lbs.	Estimated Value in Dollars in 1857 According to Cotton Price Per lb.[1]	Estimated Value in Dollars in 2020 According to Cotton Price Per lb.[2]
Amon (driver)	798	$95.76	$2,841.05
John	1,006	$120.72	$3,581.57
Big George	727	$87.24	$2,588.27
Little George	762	$91.44	$2,712.88
Jim	90	$10.80	$320.42
Edmond	768	$92.16	$2,734.24
Hampton	302	$36.24	$1,075.18
Adam	1,133	$135.96	$4,033.71
Daniel	763	$91.56	$2,716.44
Frederic	729	$87.48	$2,595.39
Edward	625	$75	$2,225.13
Albert	409	$49.08	$1,456.12
Violet	995	$119.40	$3,542.41
Tempe	954	$114.48	$3,396.44
Caroline	820	$98.4	$2,919.37
Martha	820	$98.4	$2,919.37
Pharaby	897	$107.64	$3,193.51
Minden	308	$36.96	$1,096.54
Cely	0	$0	$0
Esther	597	$71.64	$2,125.44
Harriet	420	$50.40	$1,495.29
Sarah Ann	304	$36.48	$1,082.30
Little Eliza	158	$18.96	$562.51
Ella	293	$35.16	$1,043.14

Source: McMurtry-Chubb Plantation Record Database.
[1]According to records kept by Jefferson Davis, cotton was selling at $0.12/pound by November 1857. Jefferson Davis, *The Papers of Jefferson Davis: 1856-1860*, 164 (referencing DeBow's Review, 24:190; the Vicksburg Weekly Whig, October 14, 1857; and the Natchez Daily Courier, November 27, 1857). The price dropped in October 1857 from $0.125, attributable to the Crimean War, silkworm disease, and wool shortages.
[2]For these calculations, I used the CPI inflation calculator created by Ian Webster, available here: https://www.officialdata.org/us/inflation/1857?amount=35.16

Table 3.4 Alabama Enslaved Tax Assessment Guide (1848)

Age Range	Assessed Value
Under ten years of age	$175
Ten to twenty years of age	$475
Twenty to thirty years of age	$550
Thirty to forty years of age	$400
Forty to fifty years of age	$250
Fifty to sixty years of age	$100

Table 3.5 Comparison of Age, Sex, Assessed Value, and Cotton Production for Each Enslaved Person on the Joseph M. Jaynes Plantation (MS) in 1857

Name	Age	Sex	Assessed Value for 1857[1]	Total Amount of Cotton Produced in lbs. for the Week of November 22, 1857	Estimated Value in Dollars in 1857 According to Cotton Price Per lb.	Dollar Value Needed Per Week to Meet Assessed Value for 1857/lb. of Cotton[2]
Edmond	35	M	$1,100	768	$92.16	$21.15	176
Big George	31	M	$1,200	727	$87.24	$23.07	192
Amon(driver)	28	M	$1,200	798	$95.76	$23.07	192
John	28	M	$1,200	1,006	$120.72	$23.07	192
Frederic	27	M	$1,500	729	$87.48	$28.84	240
Jim	27	M	$1,200	90	$10.80	$23.07	192
Little George	22	M	$1,200	762	$91.44	$23.07	192
Hampton	20	M	$1,200	302	$36.24	$23.07	192
Daniel	18	M	$1,200	763	$91.56	$23.07	192
Adam	18	M	$1,200	1,133	$135.96	$23.07	192
Edward	15	M	$1,000	625	$75	$19.23	160
Albert	12	M	$900	409	$49.08	$17.30	144
Minden	45	F	$500	308	$36.96	$9.61	80
Cely[3]	32	F	$1,000	0	$0	$19.23[4]	160
Tempe	33	F	$1,050	954	$114.48	$20.19	168
Martha	24	F	$1,050	820	$98.40	$20.19	168
Violet	24	F	$1,050	995	$119.40	$20.19	168
Pharaby	22	F	$1,050	897	$107.64	$20.19	168
Caroline	17	F	$1,050	820	$98.40	$20.19	168
Little Eliza	16	F	$1,050	158	$18.96	$20.19	168
Ester	14	F	$1,000	597	$71.64	$19.23	160
Harriet	11	F	$850	420	$50.40	$16.34	136
Sarah Ann[5]	10	F	$650	$710	304	$36.48	$12.50[6]	104
Ella[7]	8	F	$500	$600	293	$35.16	$9.61[8]	80

Sources: The Cotton Plantation Record and Account Book, No. 1, "I" & "C."
McMurtry-Chubb Plantation Database.

*Cotton Production is for the week of November 22, 1857 only.

[1] Enslaved persons listed are those who worked in Spring Field.

[2] I arrived at the values in this column by dividing the enslaved's assessed value by 52 (a number of weeks in a year), and then dividing that number by $0.12 (the price of cotton as of November, 1857). Jefferson Davis, *The Papers of Jefferson Davis: 1856–1860*, 164. The poundage of cotton calculated at this rate is high, because the enslaved worked six days of week, rather than seven. Also, it is possible that they did not work a full fifty-two weeks out of the year.

[3] Cely's assessed value decreased from the beginning of the year to the end of the year. The Planter's Annual Record of his Negroes upon the Plantation, made at the commencement and at the close of the year 1857, JMJPJ.

[4] At an assessed rate of $500, Cely would need to pick 80 pounds of cotton per week valued at $9.61 per week. The Planter's Annual Record of his Negroes upon the Plantation, made at the commencement and at the close of the year 1857, JMJPJ.

[5] Sarah Ann's assessed value increased from the beginning of the year to the end of the year. The Planter's Annual Record of his Negroes upon the Plantation, made at the commencement and at the close of the year 1857, JMJPJ.

[6] At an assessed rate of $710, Sarah Ann would need to pick 114 pounds of cotton valued at $13.65 per week. The Planter's Annual Record of his Negroes upon the Plantation, made at the commencement and at the close of the year 1857, JMJPJ.

[7] Ella's assessed value increased from the beginning of the year to the end of the year. The Planter's Annual Record of his Negroes upon the Plantation, made at the commencement and at the close of the year 1857, JMJPJ.

[8] At an assessed rate of $600, Ella would need to pick 96 pounds of cotton valued at $11.54 per week. The Planter's Annual Record of his Negroes upon the Plantation, made at the commencement and at the close of the year 1857, JMJPJ.

Avery [busy?] rain last night-Ginning-Picking-cutting up boys in spring field scraping up manure in [?] My child is no better Dr [?] stayino[sic] [?] last night [. . .] Finished Ginning-[?] yesterday corn increased Ginning for Wright [?] this morning Edmon Ginning Amon an[sic] Jim Digging-Grave The balance cutting boys scraping up manure Mary Ann Alliston departed this life half-passed eight o'clock this morning [.][155]

Of the nineteen enslaved men and women in his care, Levy knew what each was doing on a daily basis.[156] His recording and managing slave labor consumed so much of his time that he mentioned the death of his child and the digging of her grave as just another entry in the long list of accomplished work.

Alliston Levy's case is a cautionary tale on the limits of overseer patriarchal control and masculine authority. Statutes, contracts, and plantation management schemes all worked together to subvert overseer control of their time and judgment to planters like Joseph M. Jaynes' social and economic interests. Plantation management limited how overseers like Levy were able to exercise their independence and freedom as White men. That Levy documented enslaved labor practices was of more pressing concern for Jaynes than Levy's exercise of paternalism for his sick and ailing child. To be sure, planters were not able to commoditize an overseer child's labor in the same manner as enslaved child labor in the plantation economy. The penalty planters exacted from overseers for failing to drive enslaved men and women to peak productivity were their wages—wages that could lead to land and enslaved of their own. Even more, the terms of their contracts with planters subjected overseers to a loss of their full rights as White men—chief among them independence, allocation of their time and labor, and bodily control.

NOTES

1. Bill Cooke, "The Denial of Slavery in Management Studies," *Journal of Management Studies* 40, no. 8 (December 2003): 1895, 1900. Cooke argues that the number of overseers is linked to "plantations merging, (bigger plantations, fewer owners, more managers—hence an increasing separation of ownership and control) and the expansion of slavery in to 'new' parts of the western U.S. Accordingly, the number of plantations with more than one hundred people who were slaves had increased to 2,279 by 1860" (from the 1,449 in 1850 cited by [Alfred D.] Chandler [*The Visible Hand: The Managerial Revolution in American Business* (Cambridge: Harvard University Press, 1977)]). Cooke, "The Denial of Slavery in Management Studies," 1911. For more on the southwest expansion of enslavement and the internal trade in enslaved labor, see Beckert, *Empire of Cotton: A Global History*, 109; Baptist, *The Half Has Never Been Told*, 113. This explanation for the explosion of

plantation management is contradicted by Gray. He argues that although after the colonial period, innovations in agriculture began to evolve, the economic depression in the 1850s provided a strong catalyst for planters to re-think the management of their plantations. Gray and Thompson, *History of Agriculture: Volume I*, 546; Lewis Cecil Gray, *History of Agriculture in the Southern U.S. to 1860: Volume II* (New York: A.M. Kelley, 1973), 779. Such concern was even more prevalent after the depression when enslaved labor was very expensive and planters became increasingly concerned with how they were being treated. Gray and Thompson, *History of Agriculture: Volume I*, 546. Gray states, "[many] planters undertook to get along entirely without overseers, or to superintend in person the policy of management, employing overseers merely to execute details. The old maxim 'The master's footsteps are manure to his land,' acquired an increased emphasis during this period." Gray and Thompson, *History of Agriculture: Volume I*, 547. Given the hard data Cooke, Chandler, and Scarborough (whom Chandler cites) provide for the increase in plantation size and management, Gray's claims of overseer decrease seem to be rooted in paternalist notions about the treatment of the enslaved. That punishment and torture of the enslaved was necessary to plantation management and productivity undermines his claims. See Frederick Law Olmsted, *The Cotton Kingdom: A Traveller's Observations on Cotton and Slavery in the American Slave States, 1853–1861* (2017), 417, Kindle. Olmsted writing in the same period as Gray noted in his observations of one plantation that the enslaved from two plantations had been merged, resulting in workforce of 200 enslaved.

2. Beckert, *Empire of Cotton: A Global History*, 110; Cooke, "The Denial of Slavery in Management Studies," 1897–1898.

3. Beckert, *Empire of Cotton: A Global History*, 110.

4. Ibid.

5. Ibid, p. 109; Baptist, *The Half Has Never Been Told*, 113.

6. Baptist, *The Half Has Never Been Told*, 113, 116; Johnson, *River of Dark Dreams*, 180–82.

7. Baptist, *The Half Has Never Been Told*, 83, 113; Beckert, *Empire of Cotton*, 104–105.

8. Baptist, *The Half Has Never Been Told*, 112–113, 116–117; Beckert, *Empire of Cotton*, 115.

9. Baptist, *The Half Has Never Been Told*, 112–113, 116; Bill Cooke, "The Denial of Slavery in Management Studies," 1897–1898; Beckert, *Empire of Cotton*, 115.

10. Beckert, *Empire of Cotton*, 115; Baptist, *The Half Has Never Been Told*, 116; Lea Vandervelde, *The Last Legally Beaten Servant in America: From Compulsion to Coercion in the American Workplace*, 39 Seattle U.L. Rev. 727, 768–75 (2016).

11. Baptist, *The Half Has Never Been Told*, 115–116.

12. Baptist, *The Half Has Never Been Told*, 117, 121. Frederick Law Olmsted described the gang labor organization he witnessed in the cotton fields in noting "[the enslaved are constantly and steadily driven up to their work, and the stupid plodding machine like manner in which they labour [sic] is painful to witness. This was especially the case with the hoe gangs. One of them numbered nearly two hundred hands

(for the force of two plantations was working together), moving across the field in parallel lines, with a considerable degree of precision. I repeatedly rode through the lines at a canter, with other horsemen, often coming upon them suddenly, without producing the smallest change or interruption in the dogged action of the labourers [sic], or causing one of them, so far as I can see, to lift an eye from the ground." Frederick Law Olmsted, *The Cotton Kingdom*, 417. For criticisms of Baptist's term "pushing system" to describe the system of pace setting for cotton picking, see Olmstead and Rhode, "Cotton, Slavery, and the New History of Capitalism," 1–17, 9. The authors also cite to Martin Weitzman's "ratchet principle" to suggest that punishment would likely disincentivize productivity over the long term. For more, see Martin L. Weitzman, "'The Ratchet Principle'" and Performance Incentives," *The Bell Journal of Economics* 11, no. 1 (Spring 1980): 302–308.

13. Baptist, *The Half Has Never Been Told*, 115.

14. Johnson, *River of Dark Dreams*, 171. For more on whipping used as a means to subjugate enslaved men and women, see Lea Vandervelde, *The Last Legally Beaten Servant in America*, 39 Seattle U.L. Rev. at 775–77.

15. Johnson, *River of Dark Dreams*, 249.

16. Ibid.

17. Available here: https://archive.org/details/conciseviewofsla00thom/page/n7/mode/2up

18. E. Thomas, *A Concise View of the Slavery of the People of Color in the United States* (Philadelphia: E. Thomas, 1834), Table of Contents.

19. Ibid., Preface, v.

20. Northup, *Twelve Years a Slave*, 108–109.

21. Edward E. Baptist, *The Half Has Never Been Told*, 116–117.

22. Cooke, "The Denial of Slavery in Management Studies," 1895–98.

23. Ibid., pp. 1895, 1900.

24. Solomon Northup described the hierarchy of management on plantations: "Besides the overseer, there are drivers under him, the number being in proportion to the number of hands in the field. The drivers are black, who, in addition to the performance of their equal share of work, are compelled to do the whipping of their several gangs. Whips hang around their necks, and if they fail to use them thoroughly, are whipped themselves." Northup, *Twelve Years a Slave*, 109. Drivers were also mentioned in court cases. The case *Jacob v. Ursuline Nuns* involved a lawsuit by the children of a deceased free man against an order of nuns in Louisiana for payment for services incurred by their father while employed as a driver and subsequently an overseer on their plantation. *Jacob v. Ursuline Nuns*, 2 Mart. (o.s.) 269 (1812). The children alleged that their father was a driver on the nun's plantation in Louisiana until 1796, when he was emancipated at the age of 60 (Ibid., p. 272). After that time he worked as an overseer for fifteen years until his death in 1811 at the age of seventy-five on land that the convent allegedly donated to him (Ibid., pp. 269, 272). The monk and nuns testified that none of the enslaved of age range eighteen to forty-two who worked on their plantation at any given time was free, and that the plantation was not a commercial enterprise because it existed to provide the convent with necessary produce (Ibid., pp. 272–273). Overseers at the plantation were regularly paid anywhere

from $5 to $100 each month (Ibid., p. 273). However, the deceased free driver cum overseer was never paid for his services. In considering the children's claim for the bequest, the court reasoned that since the deceased did not make any claim for overseer wages over the fifteen years he worked as free man, he gave his services as a continued act of gratitude for his freedom and for his maintenance and care at the convent (Ibid., p. 274). Because the deceased was age sixty-nine when any land was allegedly donated to him, the court opined that his labor at that point would not be worth more than his upkeep (Ibid., p. 275). The case was put to a jury to decide, who ultimately could not reach a verdict (Ibid., p. 275). See also *Harmon v. Fleming*, in which the court is critical of judicial opinions that discuss contracts for overseer labor and enslaved labor in similar terms. *Harmon v. Fleming*, 25 Miss. 135, 138–139 (1852).

25. Olmsted, *The Cotton Kingdom*, 417–418. It is also likely that Joseph M. Jaynes utilized at least one enslaved driver on his plantation. "Amon" (no last name) is listed in the space designated for the overseer's name in the overseer's account of daily cotton picked. Daily Record of Cotton Picked on Joseph M. Jaynes' Plantation, during the week commencing on the 29th day of November 1857, JMJPJ. However, he is valued on enslaved labor valuation records for 1857 at $1,200, commiserate with other enslaved men in his age group. The Planter's Annual Record of his Negroes upon the Plantation, made at the commencement and at the close of the year 1857, JMJPJ. Additionally, John Allison is listed as overseer on other plantation records documenting enslaved labor in 1857. Daily Record of Cotton Picked on Joseph M. Jaynes Plantation, during the week commencing the 1st day of November 1857. Levy Allison, a possible relation, was listed as overseer on the same records just two years prior. Daily Record of Passing Events on Joseph M. Jaynes Plantation, during the week commencing 22nd day of April 1855, JMJPJ; Daily Record of Passing Events on Joseph M. Jaynes Plantation, during the week commencing on the 29th day of April 1855, JMJPJ; Daily Record of Passing Events on Joseph M. Jaynes Plantation, during the week commencing on the 10th day of June 1855, JMJPJ.

26. Olmsted, *The Cotton Kingdom*, 418.

27. Ibid. Emphasis mine.

28. Bassett and Polk, *The Southern Plantation Overseer As Revealed in His Letters*, 28. Plowden C. J. Weston, owner of several rice plantations in South Carolina, incorporated the following terms into his overseer contracts: "No Driver, or other negro, is to be allowed to punish any person in any way, except by order of the overseer and in his presence." Bassett and Polk, *The Southern Plantation Overseer As Revealed in His Letters*, 23, 28.

29. For example, *Richardson v. Pumphrey*, which involved settlement upon the break-up of a partnership formed for the purpose of planting. 2 La. Ann. 448 (1847). In the case, the defendant appealed a judgment in amount of $2,097.30, which appears to be Pumphrey's understanding of the wages due him for managing the plantation as an overseer would (Ibid., p. 449). In describing Pumphrey's obligation to the partnership, the court describes skills White men can possess: "The defendant was the sole manager of the concern, as he has kept no regular account of his receipts and expenditures, the settlement between him and his partner can only be made by approximation.

With men of a different class, we would be disposed to consider the omission to keep books as a badge of fraud; but it is not so with overseers and persons who follow their avocations. Their education does not generally qualify them for the task" (Ibid., p. 449, emphasis mine). The court rejected Pumphrey's claim for overseer wages, stating his obligation to manage the plantation as its co-owner (Ibid., p. 449).

30. For example, Thomas D. Morris, *Southern Slavery and the Law 1619–1860* (Chapel Hill: University of North Carolina Law), 183.
31. Alabama Slave Code No. 41, § 1., 103 (1848).
32. Alabama Slave Code No. 41, § 2., 103 (1848).
33. Alabama Slave Code No. 41, § 1., 103 (1848).
34. Alabama Slave Code 390 §§ 2042, 2043 (1852). For a discussion of cruelty and humanity between masters and enslaved labor, see Jenny Bourne Wahl, *Legal Constraints on Slave Masters: The Problem of Social Cost*, 41 Am. J. Legal Hist. 1 (1997).
35. Laws of Mississippi 235 §2 Article 5 (1857).
36. For example, Genovese and Fox-Genovese argue in *Fatal Self-Deception: Slaveholding Paternalism in the Old South*, that "[from] colonial times to emancipation, southern planters behaved accordingly, blaming overseers for cruelty to slaves and projecting themselves as caring father figures." 51. See also Gross, *"Like Master, Like Man"* 18 Cardozo L. Rev. at 265. Gross argues that "[while] paternalist rhetoric was useful to help build up a master's image, it only entered into the legal doctrine at the point where the master's own behavior was not at issue—when a hirer, overseer, or agent had charge of the slave. We need to move beyond the paternalism question to understand how the law worked to establish what it meant to be master and, therefore, what it meant to be a white man in Southern plantation society." For more interpretations on planter character as revealed through litigation concerning private law matters, see Ariela J. Gross, *Double Character: Slavery and Mastery in the Antebellum Southern Courtroom* (Princeton: Princeton University Press, 2000).
37. Laws of Mississippi, 235, Ch.33, Article 4 (1857).
38. The Code of the State of Georgia 770, §51 (1831).
39. The Code of the State of Georgia 770, §52 (1831).
40. Alabama Slave Code 591 §3297 (1852).
41. Alabama Slave Code 592 §3299 (1852).
42. *Brunson v. Martin*, 17 Ark. 270, 270 (1856).
43. Ibid., p. 270.
44. Ibid., p. 275.
45. Ibid.
46. Ibid., pp. 275–276.
47. Ibid., p. 276.
48. Ibid., pp. 271, 275.
49. Ibid., pp. 270–271.
50. Ibid., p. 274.
51. Ibid.
52. Ibid.
53. Ibid.

54. Ibid.
55. Ibid., pp. 274–275.
56. Ibid., p. 275.
57. Ibid.
58. Ibid.
59. Ibid.
60. Ibid.
61. Ibid., p. 272.
62. Ibid., pp. 271–272.
63. Ibid., p. 276.
64. Ibid., p. 277.
65. *Gillian v. Senter*, 9 Ala. 395 (1846).
66. Ibid., p. 395.
67. Ibid.
68. Ibid.
69. Ibid.
70. Ibid., p. 396.
71. Ibid., pp. 396–397 (emphasis mine)
72. Ibid., p. 398.
73. Alabama Slave Code 390 §§ 2042, 2043 (1852).
74. *Womack v. Nicholson*, 3 Rib (LA) 248 (1842). An enslaved woman, Nancy, was beaten so severely that she prematurely delivered her child (Ibid., p. 248.) Womack, Nancy's owner, hired her out to Nicholson, at which time Nancy fell under the supervision of Nicholson's overseer, Churchman (Ibid., p. 248). The court ruled in favor of Womack, but only for expenses related to medical treatment and recovery (Ibid., p. 250).
75. *Martineau v. Hooper*, 8 Mart. (o.s.) 699, 700 (1820). The overseer Hooper was not liable for killing an enslaved in the act of escape (Ibid., pp. 700–701). The enslaved, Harry, was described as "ungovernable" by his master (Ibid., p. 700).
76. *Johnson v. Lovett*, 31 Ga. 187, 187, 190 (1860).
77. Ibid., p. 191.
78. Ibid., pp. 191–192.
79. Three cases handed down by the Louisiana Supreme Court serve as exemplars. In *Miller v. Stewart*, Miller, an overseer, was fired before the end of his year contract term on the Stewart plantation for cruelty toward an enslaved man, Tom. 12 La.Ann. 170, 171 (1857). Miller whipped Tom to death (Ibid.). He sued the planter, Stewart, for his pro-rated salary amount up to the time of his discharge, which he was awarded at trial (Ibid.). Stewart appealed, arguing that he was entitled to Tom's value, which the salary would off-set (Ibid.). Stewart won on appeal (Ibid,. pp. 171–172). Tom was whipped from his neck to his heels (Ibid., p. 171). Witnesses described his injuries as "stripes on him so close together that, that the witness could not put his finger between them" (Ibid., p. 171). No evidence was introduced that Tom was "vicious" or possessed a bad character (Ibid., p. 171). In *Kennedy v. Mason*, the estate of a deceased planter, Mason, refused to pay overseer, Kennedy, the balance of his wages for 1851. 10 La. Ann. 519, 519–520 (1855). The estate argued that Kennedy

58   Chapter 3

was liable for the death of the enslaved, Jim Crack, as a result of Kennedy's mistreatment (Ibid., p. 520). Jim had run away or had otherwise been absent from the plantation (Ibid., p. 520). When he was captured and returned, Kennedy stripped him, tied him face down on the ground, and beat him with a hand saw and whip (Ibid., p. 520). It was an especially cold evening (Ibid., p. 520). Kennedy left Jim in this position for approximately an hour and a half, during which time he continued the beatings intermittently (Ibid., p. 520). After this time had elapsed, Kennedy rubbed Jim with an ointment, administered castor oil orally, and sent him to his living quarters (Ibid., p. 520). Four hours later, he was found dead (Ibid., p. 520). The court found Kennedy liable for Jim's value (Ibid, p. 521). Lastly, in *Taylor v. Paterson*, the overseer, Taylor, sued the planter, Paterson, for unpaid wages due under an 1850 employment contract. 9 La. Ann. 251, 251 (1854). Taylor was fired before the end of the contract term for shooting an enslaved man, Alfred (Ibid., pp. 251, 253). Paterson alleged that Alfred's injuries resulted in lost services, costs for his medical treatment, and diminished Alfred's value (Ibid,. p. 251). The jury awarded Taylor his prorated salary amount minus an amount for Alfred's lost services (Ibid., p. 251). Paterson appealed on grounds that Taylor was not entitled to any wages because he breached his contract by shooting Alfred (Ibid., p. 251). The Supreme Court of Louisiana reversed the judgment of the lower court and remanded the case for new trial (Ibid., p. 253). See also Morris, *Southern Slavery and the Law*, 183.
   80. *Hendricks v. Phillips*, 3 La. Ann.618, 618 (1848).
   81. Ibid., p. 618.
   82. *Dwyer v. Cane*, 5 La. Ann. 707, 707 (1851).
   83. Ibid., p. 707.
   84. *Prichard v. Martin*, 27 Miss. 305, 312-13 (1854).
   85. Ibid., p. 308.
   86. 22 Ga. 545, 546 (1857).
   87. Ibid., p. 552.
   88. Ibid., pp. 552–553.
   89. Ibid., p. 551.
   90. Ibid., p. 552.
   91. Ibid.
   92. Ibid., pp. 557–558.
   93. Ibid., p. 558.
   94. Ibid., p. 559.
   95. Ibid., pp. 545–546.
   96. Ibid., p. 559.
   97. 5 Ala. 477, 478 (1843).
   98. Ibid., p. 478.
   99. Ibid.
   100. Ibid., pp. 478–479.
   101. Ibid., p. 483.
   102. See, for example, *Cox v. State*, 32 Ga. 515 (1861). The overseer, Cox, was found guilty of voluntary manslaughter for killing an enslaved man, Humphrey (Ibid., pp. 515–516). Cox appealed on grounds that the Court incorrectly declined to give

the jury an instruction on enslaved resistance as adequate cause for killing (Ibid., pp. 519–520; 521). See also, *Dowling v. State*, 13 Miss. 664 (1846). The overseer, Dowling, was convicted at the trial for killing an enslaved man, Dick Smith (Ibid., p. 665). The Mississippi Court of Appeals overturned Dowling's conviction on several grounds, among them that his treatment of other enslaved labor on the plantation should not have been admitted into evidence as proof of how he might have treated the deceased (Ibid., pp. 696–697).

103. For example, an Alabama law passed during the 1855–1856 session provided: "The more effectually to secure subordination among slaves, by requiring the owner, or overseer to reside with them. Section 1. Be it enacted by the Senate and House of Representatives of the State of Alabama in General Assembly convened, That from and after the 1st day of March, 1856, not more than six hands shall be suffered to reside on any plantation in the State of Alabama unless the owner, or overseer, or a white man, remains on the same place with them, or within the distance of a mile. Section 2. Be it further enacted, That any person violating the first section of this act, for three months consecutively, shall be liable to indictment and upon conviction shall be fined one hundred dollars, one-half of which shall go to the informer, and the other in the county treasury" (Alabama Session Law 18 No. 28, 1855–1856).

104. *Alabama:* Be it enacted by the Senate and House of Representatives of the State of Alabama in General Assembly convened. That if any master, owner, overseer, or other person having the management and control of any slave shall permit such slave to hire his, her, or their time or services to any other person, all persons so offending may be indicted for a misdemeanor, and upon conviction, be fined in a sum not less than five or more than $100, at the discretion of the jury trying the same: Provided, that the proper authorities of any corporate city or town, in this state, may grant license or permission to owners of slaves to allow their slaves to work out and hire their time by day. Alabama Legislative Acts 107 § 1 No. 46 (1848); No master, overseer, or other person having the charge of a slave, must permit such slave to hire himself to another person, or to hire his own time, or to go at large, unless in a corporate town, by consent of the authorities thereof, evidenced by an ordinance of the corporation; and every such offense is a misdemeanor, punishable by fine not less than $20 nor more than $100. Alabama Slave Code 237 §1005 (1852); *Mississippi:* If any master or employer of a slave, shall license such slave to go at large, and trade as a free man, the master or employer shall forfeit and pay the sum of $50 to the state, for the use of the literary fund; and if, after conviction, such slave shall be found going at large, and trading, the master or employer shall again be liable to the like penalty; and so, as often after conviction, as such slave shall be found so going at large and trading. If any person shall permit his or her slave, or any slave hired by him or her, to go at large, or hire himself or herself out, it shall be lawful for any person, and it shall moreover be the duty of every sheriff, deputy sheriff, coroner and constable of a county, to apprehend and carry such slave before a justice of the peace, of the county or corporation where apprehended; and if it shall appear to the justice, that such slave hath been permitted to go at large, or hire himself or herself out, he shall forthwith impose on the owner of such slave, or the person permitting him or her to go at large, or hire himself or herself out, as aforesaid a fine of not less than $20, nor more than

$100, or order the sheriff or other officer of their county, to sell every such slave for ready money, at the next court held for the said county (Laws of Mississippi, 159 § 18, 1840).

105. *Alabama:* No master, overseer, or head of a family must permit any slave to be or remain at his house, out house, or kitchen, without leave of the owner or overseer, above four hours at any one time; and for every such offense he forfeits $10, to be recovered before any justice of the peace, by any person who may sue for the same (Alabama Slave Code 237 §1006, 1852); *Mississippi:* Penalty for suffering slaves of others to remain about House or Plantation, above Four Hours without Leave; Penalty for suffering more than Five to Remain at any one time. If any master, overseer, or employer shall knowingly permit or suffer any slave or slaves not belonging to him or her, to be, and remain, in or about his or her house or kitchen, or upon his or her plantation, above four hours at any one time, without leave of the owner, overseer or employer of such slave or slaves, he or she, so permitting, shall forfeit and pay $10 for every such offence: provided, always, that nothing herein contained shall be construed to prohibit negroes or slaves of the same owner, though seated at different quarters, from meeting, with their owner's or overseer's leave, upon any plantation belonging to such owner; nor to restrain the meeting of slaves on their master's, employer's, or overseer's business at any public place, nor on any other lawful occasion, by license, in writing, from their master, employer, or overseer (Laws of Mississippi 526 § 1, 1823).

106. *Alabama:* Any owner or overseer of a plantation, or householder, who knowingly permits more than five negroes, other than his own, to be and remain at his house, plantation, or quarter, at any one time, forfeits $10 for each and every one over that number, to the use of any one who may sue for the same, before any justice of the peace; unless such assemblage is for the worship of almighty God, or for burial service, and with the consent of the owner or overseer of such slaves (Alabama Slave Code 237 §1007, 1852); *Mississippi:* Penalty for suffering slaves of others to remain about House or Plantation, above Four Hours without Leave; Penalty for suffering more than Five to Remain at any one time. And every master, employer, or overseer, who shall, without such leave permit or suffer more than five negroes, or slaves, other than those in his or her own employment, to be and remain upon his or her plantation, or quarter, at any one time, shall forfeit and pay $10 for every such negro or slave; which said several forfeitures shall be to the informer, and recoverable, with costs, before any Justice of the Peace of the county or corporation where such offence is committed: provided, always, that nothing herein contained shall be construed to prohibit negroes or slaves of the same owner, though seated at different quarters, from meeting, with their owner's or overseer's leave, upon any plantation belonging to such owner; nor to restrain the meeting of slaves on their master's, employer's, or overseer's business at any public place, nor on any other lawful occasion, by license, in writing, from their master, employer or overseer (Laws of Mississippi 526 §1, 1823); all meetings or assemblies of slaves, or free negroes or mulattoes mixing and associating with such slaves above the number of five, including such free negroes and mulattoes, at any place of public resort, or at any meeting-house or houses in the night, or at any school for teaching them reading or writing, either in the day time

or night, under whatsoever pretext, shall be deemed an unlawful assembly, and any justice of the peace of the county, or mayor or chief magistrate of any incorporated town, wherein such assemblage shall be held, wither from his own knowledge, or on the information of others, may issue his warrant, directed to the proper officer, authorizing him to enter the house where such unlawful assemblage or meeting may be, for the purpose of apprehending offenders, and dispersing the assemblage; and all slaves offending herein shall be tried in the manner hereinafter provided for the trial of slaves, and on conviction, shall be punished by not more than thirty-nine lashes on the bare back. Provided, that nothing herein contained shall be construed to prevent any master or employer of slaves from giving them permission in writing to go any place whatever, for the purpose of religious worship, provided such worship be conducted by a regularly ordained or licensed white minister, or attended by at least two discreet and respectable white persons, appointed for that purpose by some regular church or religious society (Laws of Mississippi 247 Article 51, 1857).

107. *Alabama:* No slave must go beyond the limits of the plantation on which he resides, without a pass, or some letter or token from his master or overseer, giving him authority to go and return from a certain place; and if found violating this law, may be apprehended and punished, not exceeding twenty stripes, at the discretion of any justice before whom he may be taken (Alabama Slave Code 238 §1008, 1852); if any slave go upon the plantation, or enter the house or out house of any person, without permission in writing from his master or overseer, or in the prosecution of his lawful business, the owner or overseer of such plantation or householder may give, or order such slave to be given, ten lashes on his bare back (Alabama Slave Code 238 §1009, 1852); *Mississippi:* No slave shall go from the tenements of his master, or other person with whom he lives, without a pass, or some letter or token whereby it may appear that he is proceeding by authority from his master, employer, or overseer; if he does, it shall be lawful for any person to apprehend and carry him before the a Justice of the Peace, to be by his order punished with stripes, or not, at his discretion, not exceeding twenty stripes; and if any slave shall presume to come and be upon the plantation of any person whatsoever, without leave in writing from his or her master, employer, or overseer, not being sent upon lawful business, it shall be lawful for the owner or overseer of such plantation, to give, or order such slave ten lashes on his or her bare back, for every such offence (Laws of Mississippi 513, 1798–1849).

108. *Molett v. State*, 33 Ala. 408 (1859).
109. Ibid., p. 410.
110. Ibid., pp. 409–410.
111. Ibid., p. 410.
112. Ibid.
113. Ibid., p. 409.
114. Ibid., pp. 412–413.
115. See Alabama Session Law 18 No. 28 (1855–1856).
116. See also Code of Arkansas 50 No. 41 (1861). By 1861, the Arkansas Legislature required "any person occupying a plantation with slaves be bound to have thereon a white person to oversee and maintain good order among them, provided he or she does not remain on said plantation in person, and on failure to do so, on

conviction thereof, he or she shall be fined not less than fifty nor more than one hundred dollars for each month said plantation shall be without such white person; this act to take effect and be in force from and after its passage."

117. Cotton Values, 1842–1843, JPFP.

118. Overseer Contract between Martha J. Jackson, Henry R. Jackson, and Vincent Peirson, January [19th ?], 1847, JPFP.

119. Overseer Contract, between Martha J. Jackson, Henry R. Jackson, and Vincent Peirson, January [19th ?], 1847, JPFP. Emphasis mine.

120. *Whitley v. Murray*, 34 Ala. 155, 157 (1859).

121. Ibid., p. 156.

122. Ibid., p. 157.

123. Ibid.

124. Ibid., pp. 157–158.

125. Thomas Affleck, "The Duties of an Overseer," in JMJPJ.

126. Ibid.

127. Ibid.

128. Ibid.

129. Ibid. As stated in the author's Prefatory Remarks in the second edition of his manual "To the Planter, the advantage is sufficiently manifest, of having the Overseer render him such an account of his stewardship; and he may safely infer that the overseer who hesitates to do so, having the blanks before him, merely requiring to be filled up, is unworthy of such trust." Thomas Affleck, *The Cotton Plantation Record and Account Book No. 1, Suitable for a Force of 40 Hands or Under* (New Orleans: B.M. Norman, 1847), in JMJPJ.

130. Thomas Affleck, "The Duties of an Overseer," in JMJPJ.

131. Ibid.

132. Gray, *History of Agriculture, Volume II*, 782. Affleck is mentioned in Gray with Thomas Spaulding. Both are described as "voluminous writers on miscellaneous matters of agricultural interest in the lower South." Their contribution to the literature is mentioned in tandem with the author's discussion of the evolution of agricultural innovations after the colonial period.

133. Thomas Affleck, *The Cotton Plantation Record and Account Book, No.1 Suitable for a Force of 40 Hands or Under*, in JMJPJ. The version that appears in the JMJPJ gives evidence of when the first and second editions were published, and that the book was in its fifth edition.

134. Ibid.

135. Ibid.

136. Rosenthal, *Accounting for Slavery*, 88–89.

137. Ibid.

138. Baptist, *The Half Has Never Been Told*, 100–101.

139. Ibid., p.102.

140. Caitlin Rosenthal, "Slavery's Scientific Management: Masters and Managers," in *Slavery's Capitalism: A New History of American Economic Development*, ed. Sven Beckert (Philadelphia: University of Pennsylvania Press, 2016), 75; Rosenthal, *Accounting for Slavery: Masters and Management*, 117.

141. Jefferson Davis, *The Papers of Jefferson Davis: 1856–1860*, eds., Mary Seaton Dix, Lynda Lasswell Crist (Baton Rouge: Louisiana State University Press, 1989), 164.

142. Johnson, *River of Dark Dreams*, 197.

143. Ibid.

144. Rosenthal, "Slavery's Scientific Management: Masters and Managers," 72, 75.

145. Daily Record of Cotton Picked on Joseph M. Jaynes Plantation, during the week commencing on the 22 day of November 1857, JMJPJ.

146. *Alabama:* Any person who on Sunday compels his apprentice, servant, or slave, to perform any labor, except the customary household duties of daily necessity, comfort, or charity, must for each offence be fined, by any justice of the county, $10 (Alabama Slave Code §3302, 1852); *Arkansas:* Be it enacted by the General Assembly of the State of Arkansas, That if any person shall hire, induce, or cause any slave to work or perform any manual labor on the Sabbath day, without the consent of the master, owner, or overseer, (such person) shall be deemed guilty of a misdemeanor and be indicted therefor by the grand jury, and, upon conviction, shall be fined in any sum not exceeding $20 (Code of Arkansas 19 §1, 1858); *Georgia:* If any person shall on the Lord's day, commonly called Sunday, employ any slave in any work or labor, (work of absolute necessity and the necessary occasions of family only excepted), every person so offending shall forfeit and pay the sum of ten shillings for every slave that he, she, or they shall so cause to work or labor (Code of the State of Georgia 770 No. 52, 1831).

147. Thomas Affleck, "The Duties of an Overseer," in JMJPJ.

148. Ibid.

149. "Mechanics and others of extra value, or those who from unsoundness or disability are of less value than slaves of like age or sex, shall be valued at whatever price the assessors from the best information to be obtained by them, may adjudge them to be worth" (Alabama Legislative Acts, Part I 17 §48, 1847–1848).

150. Alabama Legislative Acts, Part I 17 §48 (1847–1848).

151. "That the assessors in estimating the value of property, shall be governed by the criterion laid down in the following rules and definitions, and make their valuations conform thereto. First, the value of all property real and personal shall for purposes of taxation be its real worth in money, not what it would sell for at auction, or a forced sale" (Alabama Legislative Acts, Part I 16 §48, 1847–1848).

152. Tax Return of Henry Jackson of Clark County [illegible] Athens [GA] 1838, JPFP. The tax return specifically groups and lists enslaved persons "under 50 years of age" for taxation purposes. Similarly, the Tax Return for the Estate of Henry Jackson of Clark Country for 1841 lists enslaved men and women "under 50 years of age" (JPFP).

153. The Planter's Annual Record of his Negroes upon the Plantation, made at the commencement and at the close of the year 1857, JMJPJ; Daily Record of Cotton Picked on Joseph M. Jaynes' Plantation, during the week commencing on the 22 day of November 1857, JMJPJ.

154. Daily Record of Passing Events on Joseph M. Jaynes Plantation, during the week commencing 22nd day of April 1855, JMJPJ; Daily Record of Passing Events on Joseph M. Jaynes Plantation, during the week commencing on the 29th day of April 1855, JMJPJ; Daily Record of Passing Events on Joseph M. Jaynes Plantation, during the week commencing on the 10th day of June 1855, JMJPJ.

155. Daily Record of Passing Events on Joseph M. Jaynes Plantation during the week commencing on the 5th day of February 1854, JMJPJ.

156. Daily Record of Cotton Picked on J. M. Jaynes Plantation during the week commencing on the 27th day of August 1854, JMJPJ.

Chapter 4

White Masculinities, Private Law, and the Battle for Social Control

WHITE MASCULINITIES

Writing anonymously in the Southern Cultivator in 1846, a gentleman from South Carolina posed the question:

> Where are [good overseers] to be found? Are they to be picked up at grog shops, muster fields and political barbeques where the young men destined to be planters' agents are trained to a sufficient opinion of their abilities, and especially their vast privileges as "free, independent and equal citizens of this republic," who are not to stoop to be any man's man . . . or do any man's business unless allowed to do it after his own fashion?[1]

This man's question begs two more equally important questions: With whom did overseers share these privileges of freedom and independence? To whose business did they resist stooping? In the antebellum south, White men's obsession with independence was hailed as the "republican ideal."[2] This ideal was cut from the fabric of the "American" idea, woven through with the parallel threads of independence as an American identity and independence as the foundation of White masculinities.[3] Just as the colonies had become a country by severing ties with England, so too did its men become adults by severing ties with this tyrannical patriarch.[4] As Michael Kimmel argues in *Manhood in America: A Cultural History*, "The term manhood was synonymous with 'adulthood.' Just as black slaves were 'boys,' the White colonists felt enslaved by their English father, infantilized and thus emasculated."[5] Such characterizations of authority and masculinity carried through to the Antebellum Period where it gained additional meaning. Embodied in the republican ideal was the notion that White men remain "independent producers," and that slaves, the "degraded and dependent race," perform menial labor.[6] For White Southerners, slavery based on race was the guarantor of White liberty, whether planters, overseers, or yeoman farmers held that liberty.[7] For this brand of liberty to imbue its holder with power, however, the holder would have to be male and that male a planter. Overseers

> had inherited the slovenness that their fathers had inherited from the indented [sic] servants whom the colonists had brought over from the sodden mass of English laborers of the seventeenth century. There was nothing in their lives to induce them to throw off these limitations. They had the powers of a procounsul in a narrow province, and their subjects were the African slaves, the plantation mules, and the cattle. Sometimes they ruled, despite the vices inherent in this position, in such a way that the province smiled with plenty and contentment."[8]

Antebellum southern plantations epitomized patriarchal authority; they were the birthplace of the planter class of elites or the plantocracy. A fixture of the plantocracy was the characterization of the planter as a father figure in slave-holding communities.[9] Men outside of the plantocracy were not community fathers. To the contrary, overseers, as laborers to planters, were dependents of the planter class. The respective positions of both had implications for how each navigated the plantation and the wider community impacted by plantation life. As father figures, planters adhered to social and professional codes of conduct governed, in part, by a work ethic that controlled their interactions with other White men and each other.

The plantocracy perpetuated a work ethic that focused on "self- and social improvement," which was created by the planter class and performed by dependent White people, men and women, under plantocracy control.[10] Self and social improvement was essential to planters' representation of themselves as planters and their economic sustainability, but attainable largely through the work of White men not of their ranks.[11] This general professional directive was an articulation of the work ethic in racial and gendered terms.[12] Planters were White men who by virtue of their race and gender were able to own slaves and gain access to opportunities to own land (like Henry Jackson and his nearly 1,500 acres), and by virtue of their economic position were able to purchase both. In the realm of masculinities available in the South at this point in its history, planter masculinity was at the top of a hierarchy ordered by white supremacy, capitalism, and patriarchy; it was a hegemonic masculinity that was in and of itself an expression of white supremacy, capitalism, and patriarchy.[13] In the gendered order of plantation life, it was the planter's duty to "fill his station with dignity, and to be useful to his fellow beings."[14] For an overseer to "merit the esteem of others [he had to become] acquainted with the duties of [his] particular [profession], [occupation], or [station] in life, and discharge the duties of them in the most useful and agreeable manner."[15] These dueling masculinities would come to violent confrontation again and again on the public battlefield of the plantation. The rules for this duel were set in plantation management directives that ultimately governed the universe of contractual relations between the two. Planter Thomas Affleck's essay "The Duties of an Overseer" deserves revisiting in this regard.[16]

Widely published and found among the accounting documents on numerous plantations, Affleck's *The Duties of an Overseer* set the context for planter/overseer relations and ensured that the weapons for their dueling masculinities would not be equally matched.[17] Affleck wrote:

> Bear in mind, that you have engaged, for a stated sum of money, to devote your time and energies, for an entire year, to one object—to carry out the orders of your employer, strictly, cheerfully, and to the best of your ability; and, in all things to study his interests. This requires something more than your mere presence on the plantation, and that, at such times as suits your own pleasure and convenience.
>
> On entering upon your duties, inform yourself thoroughly of the condition of the plantation, negroes [*sic*], stock, implements, etc. Learn the views of your employer as to the general course of management he wishes pursued, and make up your mind to carry out these views fully, as far as in your power. If any objections occur to you, state them distinctly, that they may either be yielded or overcome. Where full and particular directions are not given to you, but you are left in a great measure of the exercise of your own judgment, you will find the following hints of service.[18]

Quoting George Washington in Washington's directions to his overseers:

> I do, in explicit terms, enjoin it upon you to remain constantly at home, (unless called off, by unavoidable business, or to attend divine worship, [*sic*]) and to be constantly with your people when there. There is no other sure way of getting work well done, and quietly, by negroes; for when an overlooker's back is turned, the most of them will slight their work, or be or idle altogether; in which case, correction cannot retrieve either, but often produces evils which are worse than disease. Nor is there any other mode than this to prevent thieving and other disorders, the consequences of opportunities. You will recollect that your time is paid for by me, and if I am deprived of it, it is worse than even robbing my purse, because it is also a breach of trust, which every honest man ought to hold most sacred. You have found me, and you will continue to find me, faithful to my part of the agreement which was made with you, whilst you are attentive to your part; but it is to be remembered, that a breach on one side releases the obligation of the other.[19]

Far from benign advice to the average manager, Affleck's essay is a glimpse of the gender dynamics at play between overseers and planters. Masculinity is homosocial; manhood is proved in public in relation to other men.[20] Not to be neglected "femininity," a construct separate from women, serves as a projection of what masculinity is not even as "[women] serve as a kind of currency that men use to improve their ranking with other men."[21] In the public sphere of the plantation, the directives in Affleck's essay cast plantation inhabitants as dependents and independents, managers and owners, all in racial and gendered terms. Planters were propertied White men who entrusted that property (land and enslaved labor) to other White men—all to achieve the goal of "[filling] his station with dignity, and [being useful] to his fellow beings."[22] Overseers were responsible for that property, but by being entrusted with it were also in control of the means by which their access to whiteness in the plantation economy was defined—through land and enslaved labor. They were complicit in maintaining planters' hegemonic masculinity,[23] to "merit the esteem of others [by becoming] acquainted with the duties of [the overseer profession],"[24] even as they struggled against it. Thus, it was necessary for planters to place checks on that control, lest there be no barriers to who wielded power over the same. The overseer's job was to implement the mind of the planter in the planter's absence rather than to implement his own. Accordingly, the performance of his masculinity on the plantation was via the intricate puppeteer strings of the planter as evident in overseer contracts for service.

PRIVATE LAW

Hegemonic masculinity uses othered masculinities as "a screen against which those 'complete' men [project] their fears, and in the process, [construct] this prevailing definition of manhood."[25] A foundational tenet of hegemonic masculinity scholarship is that definitions of manhood revolve around men's fears of being dominated by each other.[26] When viewed in this light, overseer contracts reflect how planters projected their fears of domination and control to create a prevailing definition of manhood protected and preserved by contractual terms. Planters alone held absolute power to control their enslaved, land, employees, and time as they desired. Overseers did not. As Affleck wrote in *The Duties of an Overseer*, "[it] is not proper that you should entertain a constant run of company at your house, incurring unnecessary expense, taking up your own time and that of the servants beyond what is needful for your own comfort—a woman to cook and wash for you, milk, make butter, and so on."[27] An overseer's time belonged to his planter employers, and they would account for all of it.

Planters created the terms, in this case those that outlined the appropriate work ethic, by which other White men from the overseer profession might access planter masculinity—the key to wealth. They spelled out those terms, implemented them, and enforced them in the words of the employment contracts between themselves and their overseers. Overseers that were not able to perform the contract terms year after year fell victims to stereotypes about their abilities—incapable managers, "unreliable and dishonest . . . cruel, drunken and licentious tyrants"[28]—and reinforced notions of their unworthiness to occupy the plantocracy. Planters, as "proponents of self-disciplined labor,"[29] could assume "that lack of property [land and enslaved] meant lack of effort; whereas lazy planters appeared to squander their advantages (wealth, leisure, authority), the propertyless poor seemed to squander their own labor, their only means of getting ahead."[30] Hegemonic masculinity and its attendant distortions shaped how planters were able to use overseer contracts as a means of social control.

Vincent A. Pierson's 1847 contract with Martha J. Jackson and Henry R. Jackson illuminates overseer contracts as the private battlefield for planters and overseers' competing masculinities. The contract states:

> At the particular request of the said Martha J. Jackson the said Vincent A. Pierson, engages to discontinue altogether, the use of ardent spirits, or any intoxicating liquor in any form, or under any name what ever, and should he unhappily be induced to resume the use of any kind of intoxicating drinks during the year 1847 he will acknowledge it to be sufficient cause, for his discharge from the employment of Martha and Henry Jackson.
>
> Most earnestly does Martha J. and Henry R. Jackson [illegible] that through divine assistance, Vincent A. Pierson will be enabled, to resist every temptation to the [illegible] use of spirits in any shape, as his right intimation of his integrity and character, and of his correct upright principles, renders her confidence in him so great that she would feel the most serious regret in being compelled to lose his services, which would be the [illegible] result, should he continue to be in habitual use of intoxicating liquor.[31]

These terms sought to curb Pierson's "natural" tendencies to abuse liquor, a characteristic imputed to overseers, thereby reinforcing the "natural" character of planters to refrain from the same.

Similarly and explicitly, Planter Haller Nutt issued to his overseers *General Rules to Govern Time of an Overseer*[32]:

1. Rise out of bed before day every morning. Go to the Quarters. See all hands out that can go—Go by the gin (if running) see things straight there—Go to the ox lot (if hauling)—and to the Barn (if ploughing)—see ox teams and ploughs started.

2. Then follow all hands to the field, and what time you can spare from attending to jobs let it be spent with the ploughs or Hoes [sic].
3. When you come home to breakfast—see that [illegible] is attending to his duties—go to the quarters—attend to all the sick—get breakfast—go to the gin (if running)—and then to the field again—attend to the sicks [sic] jobs as some hands may be at and balance of time if ploughs if ploughing—or hoes if scraping cotton or corn—or cotton pickers if picking.
4. At 12ocl come home with plough boys [sic]. See there [sic] herds [illegible]—go by the gin—go and attend to your sick again. Get dinner—back to mill or gin again—then to ox lot and barn lot. See all attended to—and see [illegible] to the field again when time. Then follow the ploughs and stay in the field until night—
5. At night follow ploughs home—see horses watered and fed—oxen watered and fed also. Notice [illegible] again—get supper—attend to sick—go to gin again—stay there until time [illegible]—or ginning (if running)—see all the fires put out—see all straight in quarters—ring the bell—then go to bed—
6. Watch the hands occasionally at night to see if all are in their place and no mischief—do this as well as you can after attending to business in daytime.
7. Sometimes your attention may be called from the field oftimes [sic]—in attending to sick, or when ginning and drying cotton.
8. To do all this you should never leave the plantation—if any business off the place send a negro—never go yourself unless important and necessary—
9. Besides this a man may find a little time to attend to stocks—if so, he should do it.
10. Let no negro [sic] come into the yard, except to get medicine or on special business. Let none go about the gin except them that work there.[33]

With each moment of daily time accounted for, these employment terms ensured that no overseer would squander his labor, the planter's means of getting ahead.

Yet another hurdle to poorer whites' entrance into the planter class, and overseer entrance into planter masculinity, was the denial of their equal access to enslaved labor and other property.[34] Although owning enslaved persons did not guarantee equality among White people, slave ownership would become, in the Antebellum Period, poorer whites' proverbial foot in the door for social mobility. Control over enslaved labor while an overseer, manual or reproductive, was quite another matter. Limitations on overseer ownership and use of the enslavedserved to demarcate planter masculinity as hegemonic masculinity; only the White men of the planter elite could have complete ownership, control, and authority over the bodies of their enslaved labor to do with as they pleased. As Thomas Affleck noted, an overseer's servants should be used only for his comfort, defined as a woman to cook, wash, milk, and do like tasks.[35] Thus, overseers' use of enslaved labor was not for their monetary gain, but to ensure that their time was not consumed by personal domestic concerns to the planter's detriment.

THE BATTLE FOR SOCIAL CONTROL

Litigation over the proper use of enslaved labor elucidates how enslaved labor to produce crops was planters' sole province and overseer labor was allocated to planters alone. Planter Botts acquired the plantation of Robert Bell in October 1839.[36] When Bell owned the plantation, he hired Nelson to serve as its overseer at a salary of $1,000 for a year term, which began on January 1, 1839.[37] Per their contract terms, Bell was to furnish Nelson with sugar and coffee, and pay him $10 a month to hire out an enslaved woman as a field hand that Nelson brought with him to the plantation.[38] When Botts took possession of the plantation in October 1839, he promptly fired Nelson, explaining he would rather replace Nelson with an overseer he chose.[39] The trial court awarded Nelson his salary, as well as $120 for the labor of the enslaved woman.[40] Botts appealed.[41] The appellate court affirmed the salary award, but not the cost of Nelson hiring out his enslaved labor. Despite Nelson's description of the enslaved woman as "a strong able-bodied field hand," the court explained, "[it] is not shown that she was actually employed as a hand; at work, and during a part of the time it appears that she was not in a situation to work or earn wages."[42] The court based its ruling in part on evidence that Nelson asked Bell to provide him with an enslaved person to cook for him—a regular, and common demand for overseers.[43] Although Bell told Nelson that he would provide him with a cook if he wanted to hire out the enslaved woman as field labor, the court took her failure to work as a cook as lack of fitness to labor outright.[44] This court ruling illustrates that under the plantation economy, the benefits of Nelson's enslaved labor could not accrue to him as long as he worked as an overseer. Utilizing the domestic labor of the enslaved woman in his charge would not place him in direct competition with Mr. Botts. Working her as field hand would.

These ideals were reflected in planter James Sheppard's contracts with his overseers. In a contract between himself and overseer Charles B. Crocker, Sheppard furnished Crocker an enslaved woman, Aley, for the specific purpose of caring for his family.[45] Similarly the contract between Sheppard and J. M. Key in 1860 provided Key with an enslaved woman, Nancy, to cook in exchange for Key's enslaved woman to work as a field hand.[46] Perhaps most telling were planters' restrictions on sexual relations between overseers and the enslaved. In his *General Rules to Govern Overseer Time*, planter Haller Nut wrote:

11. Above all things, avoid all intercourse with negro [sic] women. It breeds more trouble—more neglect—more idleness—more irascibility—more stealing—more lieing [sic] up in quarters—more everything that is wrong on a plantation than all else put together. Instead of studying or thinking about women in bed or out of bed, a man should think about what he has tomorrow or for a week ahead or for a month or year—actions to take advantage of this piece of work, or that little job. In fact such intercourse is out of the question. [It will] not be tolerated.[47]

Such provisions indicate that while both planters and overseers were White men for whom enslaved laborers could work, overseers' unlimited use of enslaved laborers owned by the planter was not a privilege of overseers. Further, sex with enslaved women was expressly limited to planters and a fixture of planter masculinity, as their physical and reproductive labor was the wealth of the plantation and thus the planter's alone. Overseer patriarchal authority was superior only to enslaved men, and even then only to a limited degree. When an enslaved man, Alfred, confessed to killing his overseer, Coleman, he was sentenced to death.[48] The Mississippi appellate court found that Alfred's confession was properly admitted at trial but excluded his wife, Charlotte's account explaining the reason for Coleman's murder.[49] Before Alfred went to find Coleman in what would be their final exchange, he learned that the overseer had raped his wife.[50]

Planters' checks on overseer violence toward the enslaved further underscored the fact that the planter held the reins of power, despite overseers' daily management of the plantation. Although limitations on overseers' ability to whip valuable enslaved labor can be understood as a logical way to protect the planter's investment in his most valuable commodity, they also served as a bright line that differentiated planter and overseer masculinities by their authorized actions. As noted previously, masculinities in the antebellum south were performed and contested publicly in the social environment of the plantation. Overseer masculinity did not include the unlimited ability to discipline a plantation's dependents, its enslaved. Although White men, and therefore set above the enslaved by virtue of their station, overseers were not plantation patriarchs. The planter was the plantation's father, imbued with the unfettered ability, duty, to enact and control the discipline of its dependents.

James P. Tarry's letters to his overseer Samuel O. Wood demonstrate this differentiation with caustic clarity. On July [18th?] 1854, Tarry wrote:

It is seemingly strange that you can not [sic] whip or correct a negro belonging to me, without its running away .... I want my negroes to stay on the plantation for I have no use for them here. ... I want you to understand-to withhold [sic] your rushing whipping [and] lashing-for I will not stand for it any longer. I mean exactly what I say and I want you to understand me as such—you are whipping my negroes more than I intend to allow any longer ... hands running away is no mark of a good manager-and I am weary [and] tired of it and want it stopped.[51]

In two other letters, Tarry reiterated to Wood that his temper should not determine the severity of the punishment given to his slaves. Regarding Wood's treatment of a slave named (Step?), Tarry expressly forbid Wood from punishing him further and commanded him to wait until he (Tarry) returned home to settle the matter.[52] Another letter about punishing the enslaved cautioned Wood to do the same about the enslaved laborer Tom. Tarry also added that "if you can not whip a negro without someone to help you I am the one to send not Charles Wood .... Generally running away on the plantations, and especially mine, is about the overseer."[53] In these few lines, Tarry reinforced to Wood that he (Tarry) was in control of the plantation and was the ultimate check on Wood's power.[54] It was Tarry's job as patriarch, not another overseer's (Charles Wood), to right overseer wrongs.[55]

Plantation management also required that overseers care for sick enslaved persons. This caretaking duty was not only a management one but also one that further differentiated planter and overseer masculinities. As foundational masculinities scholars R. W. Connell and James W. Messerschmidt argue, "Hegemonic masculinity at the regional level is symbolically represented through the interplay of specific local masculine practices that have regional significance .... A regional hegemonic masculinity, then, provides a cultural framework that may be materialized in daily practices and interactions."[56] On southern antebellum plantations, caring for sick enslaved persons was a masculine practice of overseers, not planters. In contrast, caring for the overseer's household was a feminine practice performed by enslaved women.[57] Accordingly, an overseer who failed to properly care for sick enslaved laborers not only gave the planter grounds to dissolve the employment contract, but also provided planters with someone to blame for the death and sickness of the enslaved men and women in their care. Caretaking as a masculine practice of overseers preserved planters' public representation of themselves as capable patriarchs. As Thomas Affleck remarked in his *Explanation of Slave Records and Accounts*, death, especially the deaths of newborns, was a mark of bad management.[58]

Affleck also contended that the common illnesses suffered by enslaved labor were due to overseer mismanagement. He opined that enslaved men and women's exhaustion from work, wandering around at night, exposure to rainy conditions, improper clothing, and non-nutritious badly cooked food were the cause of much illness and in the direct control of overseers.[59] Therefore, in his instructions, Affleck urged overseers to act as quasi-physicians (unless it was clearly a case they could not handle) who cared for, "cheered and encouraged" the sick.[60] In hopes of minimizing sickness among enslaved laborers, overseers were also to give alternative indoor tasks on rainy days, see that nutritious foods were fed to the enslaved workforce regularly, and to pay close attention to pregnant women and the care they gave newborns.[61] These new responsibilities placed additional caretaking burdens on overseers.[62]

Although it is not evident that all planters had knowledge of Affleck's manual, references to sick enslaved men and women and rules governing treatment of sick enslaved laborers were a fixture of plantation life.[63] As evidenced by Haller Nutt's *Directions in Treatment of the Sick*, it was imperative for overseers to take seriously their charge to attend to ill enslaved persons. Planters generally held the opinion that this task was the most important on the plantation.[64] In Nutt's view, the possibility of sickness could be greatly diminished by consistency in work habits, good hygiene, and the prevention of night wanderings. Much like Affleck's direction, Nutt cautioned that management of the sick could be an imposition and that a sick enslaved person required visiting and attendance morning, noon, and night.[65]

Despite Nutt and other planters' instructions to the contrary, courts neither equated overseer caretaking of enslaved persons, nor their diagnoses of various illnesses to a doctor's care. For example, in *Thompson v. Bertrand*, The Supreme Court of Arkansas declined to rescind a sale for an enslaved man, Albert, when his numerous overseers testified that Albert was "unsound."[66] Bertrand purchased Albert from Thompson in October 1859.[67] By April of the same year, Bertrand complained that Albert was "unsound and diseased in his knees."[68] At trial, Bertrand's overseer Hart testified that he observed Albert's knees and ankles to be "swollen and scarred" at the time Bertrand purchased him, and that Albert complained of pain in his knees during the winter months.[69] Hart deemed Albert incapable of "a good day's work."[70] During his testimony, Hart went on to speculate that Albert's illness may have been in the "small of his back" rather than his knees, but that Albert was, nevertheless, "diseased" and "unsound."[71] The court found that although Hart had sixteen years of experience as an overseer and Albert had been under his care for upwards of seven months, that Hart "[was not] a person whose reading and skill required his opinion be taken as evidence."[72] The court treated similarly the testimony of another overseer, Akin, who also testified about Albert's fitness.[73] The court deemed Akin's testimony "as the mere opinion of an incompetent person, [and] should, like the theoretical part of Hart's deposition, have been excluded from the jury upon [Thompson's] objection."[74]

In *Dupre v. Prescott*, at issue was an enslaved man, Ignace's state of health at the time of his sale through probate.[75] Ignace was sold to William Prescott on December 27, 1847, and died in April of 1848.[76] Prescott refused to pay for Ignace on allegations that Ignace suffered from heart disease prior to and through the date Prescott purchased him.[77] The estate of the late Jacques Dupre, Ignace's previous owner, sued Prescott for payment on the sale.[78] Prescott won at the trial court, and the Dupre estate appealed.[79]

Mr. Woods, Prescott's overseer, cared for Ignace from February of 1848 until his death.[80] At trial Woods testified that he observed Ignace to be in a state of illness the entire time he was under Wood's care.[81] It was only two days before Ignace died, however, that Woods called a doctor to address Ignace's complaints of chest pain.[82] Although an autopsy revealed that Ignace did suffer from heart disease, the court ruled in favor of the Dupre estate.[83] Wood's delay in calling a physician made Prescott's suit indefensible.[84]

Planters inserted courts into questions as close as whether overseers properly deemed enslaved individuals fit (healthy enough) to work, despite their protestations to the contrary. *State v. Abram*, a criminal case in the Alabama Supreme Court, considered such a cause.[85] Isaac J. Kirkendall, an overseer, saw Abram, an enslaved man, "loitering about the negro cabins" when he told Abram to get to work.[86] Abram refused, citing sickness, at which time Kirkendall felt his pulse, pronounced him well, and ordered him to work.[87] Abram "moved off slowly," but not in the direction of the fields.[88] In response, Kirkendall attempted to whip Abram, but Abram caught the whip.[89] A struggle ensued that ultimately resulted in Abram biting off part Kirkendall's ear, and Kirkendall slicing into Abram's side with a knife.[90] After sustaining his injury, the court remarked that "Abram sustained a good character, as an obedient servant."[91]

Abram challenged his indictment on grounds he was too sick to work (and therefore not required to obey any orders to work), and that the exchange between him and Kirkendall resulted in only a small bite out of Kirkendall's ear, which showed that Abram did not act maliciously.[92] A jury found Abram guilty and sentenced him to death.[93] Abram appealed.[94] The court reversed the trial court's entry of judgment and remanded the case for a new trial on grounds that Abram's intent was a factor in whether he could be found guilty of the crime charged.[95] However, the court did decide that decisions concerning whether an enslaved person is too sick to work rest in the overseer's discretion.[96] In the court's words:

> [as] a necessary consequence of the condition of slavery, as it exists with us, the master, or the overseer representing him, and clothed with his authority, must be the judge of the capacity of the slave to labor. Without this right on the part of the master, the condition of slavery does not exist, and with it, under the

protection of the law, the influence of public opinion, and the unerring suggestions of self-interest, the slave is in no danger of abuse from the cause."[97]

The court may have noted with indifference that Kirkendall's partial loss of an ear could very well end Abram's life, which was in "no danger of abuse from the cause."[98] Regardless, Kirkendall's judgment about Abram's health had a high price for the planter who owned him—Abram's new trial could have ended in his execution and therefore the planter's loss of his labor.

With the threat that courts might inject themselves into an overseer's decisions about an enslaved person's health, and possibly find him in breach of his contractual and legal obligations as an overseer, it is no wonder that treatment of the sick was ever present in his mind. Overseer letters from the Sheppard and Jackson plantations are replete with references to sick enslaved laborers. When viewed in the context of planter masculinity and the broader realm of court intervention, overseer references to sickness are about more than informing the planter about the condition of his most expensive commodity. Rather, such references provided the overseer with a way to negotiate the terms of his masculinity by salvaging himself as a capable manager—a requirement for overseer masculine identity. They further provided a way for overseers to extricate themselves from liability in their management of enslaved labor, and the inevitable dissolution of their employment contracts and subsequent lost wages, if a rampant illness was to blame.

David T. Weeks's letters to James Sheppard illustrate this point. On August 10, 1854, Weeks wrote that despite chills and fever among one-quarter of all of the enslaved laborers, he intended to get quite a bit of farm work done the next day. He also informed Sheppard that the general health of the neighborhood was the best it had ever been.[99] In a letter dated on July 8th of the same year, Weeks had assured Sheppard that "we have had no cholera nor fatal sickness here. I hear [Bass?] lost 9 negroes [and] has already had taken very bad yesterday and heard also hear [sic] that negroes are dying very fast but did not learn what the cause So I still fear our turn come next."[100] Both letters convey that Weeks was capable of managing small illnesses so that they did not severely interfere with the smooth running of the plantation. In the latter correspondence, Weeks also intimated to Sheppard that while he had succeeded in thwarting the fatal illness that had claimed many enslaved persons' lives, it would be fate and not mismanagement that brought the illness to his plantation.[101]

Similarly, Peirson wrote to Mrs. Jackson about the health and welfare of the enslaved labor in his care and his attention to their illnesses. In a letter dated November 16, 1844, Pierson told Martha about the death of the elderly enslaved woman, Betsy, and his direction to an enslaved man, Lewis, to inform him if her condition worsened through the night. He communicated to Martha in no uncertain terms that it was Betsy's sudden departure from the world and not his neglect that prevented him from visiting her before she died.[102] Such assurances by overseers to their planter superiors were necessary to convince the planters that they hired good managers who had their best interests at heart. An overseer who could provide such assurances remained in his place as a manager, a dutiful dependent to the ever-watchful patriarch. Behind every good planter was not a good woman, but a good overseer. He was the caretaker that plotted the planter's course to wealth, or drove him down the road to ruin.

NOTES

1. Bonner, "The Plantation Overseer and Southern Nationalism," 1 fn. 5.
2. Harris, *Plain Folk and Gentry in a Slave Society*, 6.
3. Michael Kimmel, *Manhood in America: A Cultural History* (New York: Oxford University Press, 2006), 13–14.
4. Ibid., 14.
5. Ibid.
6. Harris, *Plain Folk and Gentry in a Slave Society*, 6.
7. Ibid.
8. Bassett and Polk, *The Southern Plantation Overseer As Revealed in His Letters*, 7.
9. See generally Faust, *James Henry Hammond and the Old South*.
10. Joyce Chaplin, *An Anxious Pursuit: Agricultural Innovation and Modernity in the Lower South, 1730–1815* (Chapel Hill, University of North Carolina Press, 1993), 93.
11. Ibid.
12. Ibid., 129.
13. Campbell, Bell & Finney, "Masculinity and Rural Life: An Introduction," 10. The authors state that "hegemonic masculinity is . . . the version of masculinity that is considered legitimate, 'natural,' or unquestionable in a particular set of gender relations."
14. Kimmel, *Manhood in America*, 15. Note that Kimmel uses this description for the "breadwinner," who "between 1810 and 1820 [was a term] coined to denote this responsible family man" (Ibid., p. 15). Kimmel's "Genteel Patriarch" includes the planter as "breadwinner" as well (Ibid., pp. 13,14, 20). I use this description for the planter, as he is the "family man" both for the plantation as a family farm and the plantation as the capitalist enterprise of the plantocracy and plantation economy.
15. Ibid., p. 15. Likewise, Kimmel uses this description for what he calls the "Heroic Artisan," a term that includes the "independent, virtuous, and honest [man] . . . . On the family farm or in his urban craft shop, he was an honest toiler, unafraid of hard work, proud of his craftsmanship and self-reliance" (Ibid., p. 13). I apply it to

the overseer, as it encapsulates the expectations held for him as a plantation worker and his aspirations for himself.

16. Thomas Affleck, "The Duties of an Overseer," in JMJPJ.

17. For more on the popularity and use of Thomas Affleck's plantation account books, see Rosenthal, *Accounting for Slavery*, 86–89.

18. Thomas Affleck, "The Duties of an Overseer," in JMJPJ.

19. Ibid.

20. Kimmel, *Manhood in America*, 5, 30.

21. Ibid., 5.

22. Ibid., 15.

23. See Campbell, Bell & Finney, "Masculinity and Rural Life: An Introduction," 11.

24. Kimmel, *Manhood in America,* 15.

25. Ibid., 4.

26. Ibid.

27. Thomas Affleck, "The Duties of an Overseer," in JMJPJ.

28. Gray and Thompson, *History of Agriculture: Volume I*, 502.

29. Chaplin, *An Anxious Pursuit*, 93.

30. Ibid., 129. This fits nicely with Gray's hypothecation thesis. The propertyless poor could not cash in on the future value of their own labor. Gray, *History of Agriculture: Volume I*, 302, 409–410.

31. Overseer Contract between Martha J. Jackson, Henry R. Jackson, and Vincent A. Peirson, January [19th ?],1847, JPFP.

32. General Rules to Govern Time of an Overseer, n.d., HNP-JAP.

33. Ibid.

34. Chaplin, *An Anxious Pursuit*, 131. It is important to note that Chaplin makes this point to emphasize that White people in the colonial period were conflicted over the choice of enslaved labor and how their failure to expand enslavement adversely affected poor White people. Chaplin, *An Anxious Pursuit*, 182–83.

35. Thomas Affleck, "The Duties of an Overseer," JMJPJ.

36. Nelson v. Botts, 16 L.A. 596, 597 (1841).

37. Ibid., pp. 596–597.

38. Ibid., p. 597.

39. Ibid.

40. Ibid., p. 598.

41. Ibid.

42. Ibid., pp. 599–600.

43. Ibid., p. 598.

44. Ibid., pp. 598, 599.

45. Overseer Contract between James Sheppard and Charles B. Crocker, July 12, 1844, JSP.

46. Overseer Contract between James Sheppard and J.M. Key, July 23, 1860, JSP.

47. General Rules to Govern Time of an Overseer, n.d., HNP-JAP.

48. Alfred v. State, 8 George 296, 297 (1859).

49. Ibid., p. 298.

50. Ibid., pp. 298–299.

51. Letter from James P. Tarry to Samuel O. Wood, July [18th], 185[2?], SOWP. See also Thomas Affleck, "The Duties of an Overseer," in JMJPJ. Affleck cautioned them that using the whip too much to "correct" enslaved laborers was both "unnecessary and inexcusable".

52. Letter from James P. Tarry to Samuel O. Wood, November 27,1853, SOWP.

53. Letter from James P. Tarry to Samuel O. Wood, February 6, 1853, SOWP. Other letters from this collection suggest that in addition to acting as an overseer from time to time, Samuel Wood also traded/sold enslaved labor, and might have even worked as a cotton factor. Letter from C. Billingsley to Samuel Wood re the sale of an "unsound" enslaved boy Elijah, May 10, 1859, SOWP; Letter from James P. Tarry to Samuel O. Wood, December 8, 1855, SOWP. Six years after Tarry's letter to Wood about Tarry's enslaved man, Tom, Tarry addresses Wood as "Esq.," suggesting at least at this point Wood owns some land. Letter from James P. Tarry to Samuel O. Wood, August 9, 1859, SOWP.

54. See also Faust, *James Henry Hammond and the Old South*, 100. In the author's words, "Hammond emphasized to his deputies that the necessity for frequent flogging was certain evidence of poor management. Whipping, he explained, was a last resort, to be turned to when other techniques of control had failed. Hammond advised a new overseer that he would evaluate his performance 'by the success in promoting industry without flogging.' "

55. Letter from Mary [C.?] Wood to Samuel O. Wood, October 29, 1855, SOWP. In this letter from Samuel's mother, Charles (Charley) is specifically mentioned. He is also distinguished from Charles Tarry, as he is mentioned separately in the same letter. The Tarrys, for the most part, are planters; the Woods, even though related to them, are not.

56. Connell and Messerschmidt, "Hegemonic Masculinity: Rethinking the Concept," 849–850.

57. For example, Thomas Affleck, "The Duties of An Overseer," in JMJPJ.

58. Thomas Affleck, "Explanation of Slave Records and Accounts," in JMJPJ. See also Directions in treatment of the sick, HNP-JAP. In Nutt's opinion, "If a woman miscarrie[d], which should never be in the case on a well managed plantation . . . there is something wrong-she has been badly managed-worked improperly." James Henry Hammond went so far as to reward his overseers $10 for every slave birth that exceeded the number of slave deaths. Faust, *James Henry Hammond and the Old South*, 126.

59. Thomas Affleck, "Duties of an Overseer," in JMJPJ. Note: A enslaved person's depreciation in value was also said to be the cause of overseer mismanagement. See Thomas Affleck, "Explanation of Records and Accounts," in JMJPJ.

60. See also Directions in Treatment of the sick, HNP-JAP. There is no doubt that Nutt expected his overseers to be quasi-physicians. Contained in his directions are detailed instructions on how to treat everything from fevers to snakebites, what medicine to administer, and how it should be administered.

61. Thomas Affleck, "The Duties of an Overseer," JMJPJ.

62. Such instructions seem to be quite typical. For example, Gray quotes a set of instructions to a Louisiana overseer that almost mirror Affleck's. Gray, *History of Agriculture: Volume I*, 547. See Breeden, *Advice Among Masters*.

63. Joyce Chaplin argues at length in *An Anxious Pursuit* that sickness was a rite of passage into plantation life among White people in the Lower South (Ibid., pp. 93–96). Chaplin explains that these White people spent a lot of time trying to combat illness by naturopathic means, and that they believed even severe illnesses (e.g., malaria) were not sufficient to excuse plantation mismanagement (Ibid., p. 97). More importantly, Chaplin also points to the class divisions that were exposed by planters' reaction to sickness. In her words, "Some precautions were luxuries beyond the reach of many residents, and, while the elite removed themselves from the worst dangers, the poor stayed behind to face them armed only with their acquired resistance and a good bolus of bark" (Ibid., p. 98). These points are significant especially when viewing them in the context of Affleck's advice and Nutt's instructions. Affleck wrote specifically for the Lower South and Nutt's plantation was located in Mississippi.

64. Directions in treatment of the sick, HNP-JAP.

65. Ibid. It is likely that Affleck influenced Nutt because his plantation was in Mississippi like Jaynes'. If Jaynes had a copy of Affleck's management tools, it is likely that Nutt would have had one also. Even if this is not true, there is no reason to disbelieve that Nutt was among the planters who were making agricultural innovations. The presence of instructions to his overseer is evidence that he governed his overseers, if only in part, by written directives.

66. Thompson v. Bertrand, 23 Ark, 730, 730–32 (1861).

67. Ibid., p. 731.

68. Ibid.

69. Ibid., p. 732.

70. Ibid.

71. Ibid.

72. Ibid., pp. 732–733.

73. Ibid., p. 733.

74. Ibid.

75. Dupree v. Prescott, 5 La. Ann. 592, 593 (1850).

76. Ibid., p. 593.

77. Ibid., pp. 592–593.

78. Ibid., p. 592.

79. Ibid., p. 593.

80. Ibid.

81. Ibid.

82. Ibid.

83. Ibid.

84. But see *Lynch v. McRee*, 18 La. Ann 640 (1866) where the sale of an enslaved boy, Frank, was annulled because the overseer called in a doctor who diagnosed Franks condition within a reasonable time of sale (Ibid., p. 641). Dupre can be read as reinforcing overseer's obligations to care for sick enslaved persons by calling in a doctor when necessary. However, an overseer's obligation to call a doctor does not necessarily make the enslaver responsible for any costs incurred in treating the enslaved. For example, in *Peake v. Scaife*, the South Carolina Court of Appeals found no privity of contract between an enslaver and a doctor when the overseer, not the

enslaver, called the doctor to treat the enslaved. 11 Rich. 672, 674–675 (1858). The court ruled that the overseer was liable for the doctor's bill, not the enslaver. Ibid., p. 675.

    85. State v. Abram, 10 Ala. 928 (1847).
    86. Ibid., p. 928.
    87. Ibid.
    88. Ibid.
    89. Ibid.
    90. Ibid., pp. 928–929.
    91. Ibid., p. 929.
    92. Ibid., pp. 929, 931–932.
    93. Ibid., p. 929.
    94. Ibid.
    95. Ibid., pp. 931–932.
    96. Ibid., pp. 933.
    97. Ibid.
    98. Ibid.
    99. Letter from D. T. Weeks to James Sheppard, September 10, 1854, JSP.
    100. Letter from D. T. Weeks to James Sheppard, July 8, 1854, JSP.
    101. Ibid.
    102. Letter from Vincent A. Pierson to Martha J. Jackson, November 16, 1844, JPFP. The exact wording of the passage is as follows: "I saw the day before that she was going [and] told Lewis if she got worse in the night to tell me now [?] but she dropped off so suddenly I did not gett [sic] the word in time to see her[.]"

Chapter 5

Immoral Men, Immoral Ends, Deference as Social Death

IMMORAL MEN

While writing his *The Cotton Industry: An Essay in American Economic History* in 1897, M. B. Hammond remarked about the disposition of the overseers who had managed the bulk of the enslaved workforce just over thirty years prior.[1] Quoting the Mississippi planter W. W. Phillips, Hammond parroted, "overseers are not interested in raising children, or meat, in improving land, or improving productive qualities of seed or animals. Many of them do not care whether property has depreciated or improved, so they have made a crop [of cotton] to boast of."[2] Writing almost thirty years later, John Spencer Bassett and James Knox Polk in *The Southern Plantation Overseer as Revealed in His Letters* similarly attested that overseers lacked the vision to advance into the planter class, to "bleach out of the family all traces of the overseer taint."[3] Apparently, "the majority were men of little imagination and saw no further into the future than the contentment that came from doing well the task of the year."[4] These aspersions cast upon overseers are disproved by the terms of their employment contracts, litigation over breaches of those contract terms, and obligations imposed upon them by statutory codes and the common law.[5] However, Hammond, Basset, and Polk accurately observed that overseers were only as valuable to planters as the crop they produced and the enslaved labor they kept on the brink of alive from cultivation to harvest. Litigation about overseers' ability to manage enslaved labor and land reflect that planters and overseers were constantly testing the boundaries of their respective masculinities through their roles and responsibilities on the plantation. Stated plainly by an anonymous Georgia planter in 1844 "Happy lot is that of the overseer—for a man without education generally, and born to labor. He is well paid for playing the luxurious part of gentleman, and possesses . . . the plantation . . . with all of its means of contributing to its comfort and pleasure."[6]

Harrold was one such overseer born to labor. Acting under his direction, enslaved persons owned by his planter/employer Graham entered James King's land, destroyed crops growing there, and carried away the fencing.[7] King's estate brought suit in trespass against Graham, pursuant to statutory provisions that made the masters liable for the acts of their enslaved labor.[8] The relevant statutory provisions shifted liability away from enslavers when the enslaved were "in the employ or hire of some other person than the owner."[9] Graham argued that he was not responsible for the actions of the enslaved persons who committed the trespass, because they acted at his overseer's direction, not his.[10] The Supreme Court of Arkansas reasoned that as the owner and master of the enslaved persons, he was their employer, not the overseer, and liable for their actions.[11] Had King's estate chosen to sue Graham under a common law theory of employee negligence, it is likely that Harrold would have been liable.[12] Graham would have avoided responsibility for the actions of his enslaved labor had Harold been charged with mismanagement in the scope of his authority as overseer.

The Supreme Court of Alabama considered a similar case in *Lindsay v. Griffin*.[13] Lindsay and Griffin had adjoining farms. Some of Griffin's pigs wandered over to Lindsay's fields, and Lindsay's overseer directed his enslaved labor to remove them.[14] The enslaved injured and killed a number of pigs as they complied with the overseers order.[15] Griffin sued Lindsay in trespass *vi et armis* (trespass with force and arms) to recover for the dead and injured pigs.[16] This type of trespass suit differs from a simple trespass suit at common law, as the latter has no intent requirement other than the commission of the act of trespass. In his defense, Lindsay argued that he was not liable for trespass, because he did not authorize his overseer to direct the enslaved to remove or kill the pigs.[17] Accordingly, he requested that the court instruct the jury not to find him liable if the evidence proved the overseer acted outside of the scope of his authority.[18] The court refused, and instead instructed the jury to find Lindsay liable if the evidence proved that the enslaved were acting under the overseer's control.[19] Lindsay lost at trial an appealed. In reversing the trial court decision, the Alabama Supreme Court explained "[the] master is responsible for the manner, as to care and skill, with which his servants execute his business, and hence it is his duty to employ none but such as are careful and competent in their particular calling; but for the unlawful purposes outside of his service, and the acts proceeding from such purposes on the part of his servants, if he does not know of, or in any manner participate in them, he is not responsible."[20]

These two cases demonstrate that for overseers, their "control" of a planter's land and enslaved amounted to a planter's temporary transfer of authority to the overseer for limited circumstances. The overseers in these cases owned no land and no enslaved—as the laboring class subservient to planters, as men born to labor, they had no claim to employing the enslaved labor force, and no liability beyond the terms of their agreements. They had no "duty" as defined in the terms of planter masculinity, but only as much authority granted to them by the planter, which was limited by their low status as White men. In the first case, Graham's transfer of authority to Harrold occurred within the scope of his work, and therefore was limited by the bounds of competence and skill necessary for Harrold to fulfill certain work tasks. Because Harrold had no claim to employing the enslaved, any directives he issued to them that implied an employee/employer relationship were void. In the second case, Lindsay's unnamed overseer had Lindsay's authority to the extent he acted competently and skillfully in discharging work duties, and refrained from intentionally inflicting harm.

Overseers "playing the luxurious part of gentleman" often emerged in situations where directives concerning the enslaved that were the logical extension of overseer authority were contrary to planter's allocations of enslaved labor. *James v. Clarke County* is such a case.[21] In the antebellum era, the roads were maintained by enslaved persons whose labor was appropriated from plantations for the public good. Statutory provisions set the requirements for legal notice to planters of the state's intention to use their enslaved labor. *James* involved a dispute over one such notice provision in the Alabama code.[22] James owned seven enslaved persons whose labor the state wished to appropriate from James's plantation to work on the public roads.[23] James's overseer received written notice two days prior to when the enslaved were due on the roads, and notified James of the same.[24] James told the overseer not to send the enslaved men to the roads.[25] The trial court subsequently enforced a penalty for default against him for failure to fulfill his statutory duty as a taxpayer.[26] James appealed the judgment, arguing that because he was not personally served with notice he could not be in default.[27] The Supreme Court of Alabama agreed, reasoning that notice to James's overseer was not the same as notice to James, and insufficient to find him in default of the statute.[28] It reversed the judgment against James and remanded the case to the trial court.[29]

While superficially simplistic, this case reveals a complexity in the boundaries of overseer/planter relationships. Had the court found James liable under the terms of the statute, it would have implied that the overseer had the authority to overrule James's decisions with respect to how he chose to use his enslaved labor. As part of the community of paternal fathers in his community, fellow planters, James's duty as a taxpayer could be invoked to override his desired allocation for his enslaved labor only when he was given notice personally, from the county. An overseer could speak with the authority a planter granted him to manage the enslaved, but could not speak for the planter in matters concerning them.

Even when a planter granted an overseer the authority to manage the enslaved, that authority flowed from planters' ownership, because ownership imposed a duty upon him. Questions of who owned the enslaved labor at any given time created uncertainly with respect to overseer authority. The case of *Porter v. Thomas* is instructive here.[30] Charles Porter was the overseer for the seventy-eight enslaved men and women owned by Henry P. Jones.[31] When Jones died, however, the executors (also heirs/beneficiaries) of his estate held the enslaved.[32] They were not in Porter's possession and only under his control so far as he was employed as Jones's overseer.[33] Jones had acquired the enslaved persons through his marriage to Mary Fulwood.[34] Mary came to own the enslaved through a bequest made to her by her first husband, John Fulwood.[35] When her second husband, Henry Jones, died, she held the enslaved in trust until her death, at which time they would be dispersed to Henry's heirs as specified in his will.[36] Mary Fulwood Jones also executed her will, in which she bequeathed the same property named in Henry's will.[37] At the time of her death, Francis Thomas was the only qualifying executor of Mary's estate.[38] Francis set out to possess the enslaved persons named in the will, who were residing on a plantation in Laurens County, Georgia, and under their overseer Charles Porter's control.[39] Henry Jones, his executors, and heirs all lived in Burke County.[40]

Thomas sued Porter in trover (wrongful detention of property) in an effort to return the enslaved to him as his property per Mary's bequest.[41] The Supreme Court of Georgia found Porter liable, reasoning that even if his possession of the enslaved was within the scope of his authority as overseer to Henry Jones' and his executors, detaining the enslaved was still a wrongful act.[42] It upheld the trial court's judgment against Porter for $46,900, the value of the enslaved, which he could satisfy by returning them to Thomas.[43] Porter was also ordered to pay Thomas $5,701.25, in payment for hiring out the enslaved.[44] Because Porter was not legally in possession of the enslaved, he had to pay for their use on the plantation where he acted as their overseer.

Although Porter was Henry's overseer (and therefore Mary's), the court was only concerned with the disposition of the property at the time of her bequest. Porter was taking care of the enslaved rightly left in his charge. If he would have failed to take care of them, Thomas would have an action against him for mismanagement. *Porter v. Thomas* is a tragic tale about the limits of authority and the duties imposed by ownership as they play out in the struggle between planter and overseer masculinities. Porter's ignorance of who owned the property he managed did not extend his authority beyond what the rightful owner was willing to give. Mary Fulwood Jones gave Porter no authority, so he was left without it. At her death, another White man of Henry's status and social standing, Francis Thomas, was the owner of Mary's enslaved and the sole decision-maker as to whom he would give their control.

IMMORAL ENDS

Planters' creation of moral standards for their overseers' created another boundary to overseers' social mobility. When searching for jobs, overseers also had to prove their "morality" and agree to refrain from "immoral" practices in contractual agreements with planters.[45] Their moral failings were not their fault; they were just born that way. As Bassett and Polk noted, "[the] overseers had the vices common to the class in society from which they sprang, the small farmers and the landless whites. They had little education, as their fathers before them had. They often drank spiritous liquors to excess, or were idle and ineffective."[46] Overseers were commonly regarded as "a perverse generation of men," with those among them, "intelligent gentlemen" who "know what their duties are and have the courage and faithfulness to perform them."[47] Because of their perceived immorality and intractability, it was necessary for overseers to be represented or represent themselves as morally upstanding persons who were capable of carrying out the obligations imposed on them by plantation management. Planters were cautious when hiring overseers and often checked around with their peers to determine the credibility of their applicants.[48] The definition of morality, at least between overseers and planters, was constructed by contractual terms, plantation management, manuals, and private law, which was designed and implemented by planters. These items "created" negative social behavior attributable to overseers and served to set them apart as the social "other" from their planter employers, and that the latter attempted to regulate.

A letter sent to Mrs. Martha J. Jackson in October 1841 by a man seeking employment as an overseer highlights the importance of representing to potential planter employers that the applicant, in this case Mr. James A. [Tunnavant?], met plantocratic standards for character and morality.[49] James spent the body of the letter explaining his experience and ended with an inquiry about wages. Below the applicant's signature was the following: "We the undersigned do recommend Mr. [Tunnavant?] as being a sober study and industrious man and a good manager on the farm [signed] [?] Elam, Byrd Pruitt, Jeremiah Jackson, [and] John Davenport"[50]

Vincent A. Peirson's 1847 contract with Martha J. Jackson and Henry R. Jackson also indicates that the character of the man who would be overseer was of upmost importance. Martha Jackson was particularly concerned with Peirson's sobriety. As a condition of the contract, he was required to completely refrain from drinking alcoholic beverages or risk dismissal from the job.⁵¹ The document states further:

> Most earnestly does Martha J. Jackson trust that through divine assistance, Vincent A. Peirson will be enabled, to *resist every temptation to the renewed use of spirits in any shape*; as her high estimation of his integrity and character, [and] of his correct upright principles; renders her confidence in him so great that *she would feel the most serious regret, in being compelled to lose his services; which would be the necessary result, should he be in the habitual use of intoxicating liquors.*⁵²

Moreover, Peirson's contract required that he show the enslaved persons on the plantation, by example, a sizable concern for his work and the prosperity of the plantation. The wording of the contract suggests that his demonstrated interest in his work should cause the enslaved labor to "make every necessary exertion" in their work on the plantation.⁵³

Comparable contractual terms appear in an overseer agreement between Thomas E. Senoir and James Sheppard signed on January 2, 1847. It stated that "Thomas E. Senoir has voluntarily and of his own accord agreed to bind himself not to [?] any intoxicating liquor during the year; and that if he [does] break this pledge he is to lose his situation and to forfeit his wages."⁵⁴ In Senoir's case, loss of his "situation" meant food promised to his family, a horse to ride, and $300.⁵⁵

Even Thomas Affleck instructed overseers to refrain from the use of liquor on the plantation, as well as to conduct Sunday religious services.⁵⁶ In his opinion the direction of enslaved laborers' moral and religious development would help to eliminate their bad behavior.⁵⁷ However, Affleck's directive about how overseers were to act was not limited to their treatment of enslaved labor. The author even went so far as to suggest how overseers should order their leisure time. In the author's view, it was not correct behavior for an overseer to entertain constantly and make unnecessary expenditures for this purpose. Such actions would consume too much of his time and put an overseer's servants to a use for which they were not intended.⁵⁸

All documents, the "resume," contracts, and Affleck's manual demonstrate the invasiveness of planter's moral standards into the lives of overseers. They also provide many insights into the role planters played in circumscribing overseers' social spaces. While it is reasonable for any employer to expect trustworthiness from an employee who is charged with managing a large capital investment, these documents represent more than adequate proof that the overseers were capable of performing their work responsibilities. If proper credentials were the sole determinant of a qualified laborer, then Mr. (Tunnavant?)'s explanation of his experience in the area and references that he was a "good manager" and "industrious man" would have been sufficient to secure the job.[59] To the contrary, an exploration into his, Peirson's, and Senoir's moral character was also an expected portion of the application process.[60] Requirements of sobriety, leadership of enslaved persons through example, integrity, and character show that the plantocracy, like Mrs. Jackson and Mr. Sheppard, held a "high estimation" of their overseers "correct [. . .] upright principles."[61]

Furthermore, Martha Jackson's use of "correct" in representing her interests in the employment contract implies that there were also incorrect principles that overseers could possess. The same can be said of the "proof of sobriety" among (Tunnavant?)'s references in his letter, and Senoir's contract. James Sheppard, and Martha and Henry Jackson's preconditions of morality in their employment contracts to Senoir and Peirson consequently served as an attempt to shape the boundaries of the overseers' social behavior in accordance with the planters' definition of virtuousness if the overseers opted for employment. These morality provisions also provided for both overseers' dismissal if their actions did not comply.

By comparison, no precondition of righteousness explicitly followed Henry R. Jackson in his pursuit of the office of Solicitor General for the Chatahoochy Circuit in Georgia.[62] In a letter to a friend of her deceased husband regarding Henry's political pursuit, Martha wrote:

> I know not of any objection that could be advanced against Henry, but his not having resided for any length of time in the circuit. This I think would be readily obviated, by its being made known that he was examined [and] admitted to the bar in Columbus, [and] commenced his practice there in the winter of 1840.[63]

Other letters written about Henry's pursuit of politics evidence further that explicit inquiries into Henry's character and sobriety were not the concerns of those who promoted his bid for solicitor. For example, Wilson Lumpkin's letter to Henry simply stated, "whatever I may have in my power, to say or do, calculated to promote your interest—and which I may consider consistent with propriety, [and] my ability to myself [and] others, *shall be done*."[64] For Lumpkin and Martha Jackson, conveyances of qualification for office or inquiry into character were not their decided concerns.[65] It is quite possible that for this group of people, such moral standards were already assumed.[66]

DEFERENCE AS SOCIAL DEATH

Connected with the prerequisite that overseers present themselves as moral persons was also the requirement that they show their respect and concern for the planter's property and the outcome of the crop. Far from a laudatory ideal, this requirement placed overseers' deference on trial in the courts, and subjected them to a possible loss of wages through breach of contract actions. In *Prichard v. Martin*, the Mississippi Supreme Court considered whether an overseer possessed the appropriate level of respect for his planter's property.[67] Martin contracted to work as an overseer on Prichard's plantation for a year.[68] Under the terms of the contract, Prichard agreed to provide Martin with coffee and sugar, his family with various resources, and Martin with a salary of $400.[69] However, Prichard fired Martin before the end of the contract term on grounds that he abused the enslaved labor and behaved disrespectfully to him.[70] At trial, nearby planters testified that Martin was "industrious and attentive to [Prichard's] business," was generally with the enslaved labor, and was never seen mistreating them.[71] Additional witnesses testified that "the plantation was always in good order and condition under his management; [and] that the horses and mules were in good condition as they usually were."[72]

The exchange that ended in allegations that Martin disrespected Prichard involved directions to enslaved labor.[73] Prichard ordered an enslaved man to move some cotton bales that could possibly have caused injury.[74] When Martin saw what the enslaved man was doing, he ordered him to stop and finish up a task to which Martin had previously directed him.[75] Martin then told Prichard that the enslaved ploughmen would move the bales when they returned from the field in two hours, and that the enslaved man who Prichard directed to that task could not have done so alone because he was elderly.[76] In the conflict that ensued, Martin told Prichard that "he had never abused the property, but had done his duty, and would not worship [Prichard]."[77]

In upholding the trial court's award of Martin's salary, the Mississippi appellate court opined that under ordinary circumstances, an overseer's disobedience of a planter's direct order would be considered "'imprudent and reprehensible', and [if] intended to set at defiance the authority of the proprietor, or done in such a manner to produce insubordination among the slaves, it would be altogether reprehensible."[78] Because another planter who witnessed the exchange continued to vouch for Martin's good character, his appropriate deferential behavior, a ruling in his favor was warranted.

More important still was that overseers demonstrate their respect for planter property, especially when their payment was part of the plantation profits. Although the possible economic return was great, overseer success bound up their subservient position to planters in perpetuating planter wealth. This was true simply because competent management by the overseer, good climate, and favorable market conditions would generate substantial economic returns for the planter. These phenomena, as reflected by overseer correspondence and contracts to Martha J. Jackson and James Sheppard, inadvertently relegated overseers to a space where deference to planter class position was part and parcel of their job as overseers.[79] Perhaps best summed up by Thomas Affleck, the overseer was to "endeavor to take the same interest in everything upon the place as if it were [their] own; indeed the responsibility in this case is greater than if it were your own, having been entrusted to you by another. Unless you feel thus, it is impossible that you can do your employer justice."[80]

Peirson's contract directed that, "[He] [show] to the Negroes *by his course of conduct, the great interest taken by himself, in the crop and general welfare of the plantation.*"[81] Letters to Martha J. Jackson throughout the year 1844 confirm the fulfillment of that particular contractual term. Writing to Martha on July 14, 1844, Peirson assured her that the crop was doing well enough for him to remove eight of the field hands to other tasks.[82] In another letter, dated September 7 of the same year, Peirson reported to Martha that he "did not sell the cotton from the fact that [he] could not get a fair offer for it."[83] In both examples, Peirson simultaneously showed his managerial agricultural skill by lessening the number of hands needed, as well as his personal investment in the monetary return on the crops by waiting for a better price.

Sheppard made either total or partial payment of some overseers' salaries contingent upon the amount of cotton produced under their supervision. Parker Carradine's contract with Sheppard in 1840 provided that he was to pay Carradine "five hundred dollars a year in good [faith?] currency of this state and five dollars per bale for all bales over above one hundred that he makes this year allowing each [bale] [weigh?] four hundred and twelve pounds."[84] Similar provisions existed in Asa Kemp's contract of 1841 and David T. Weeks contract of 1856. Sheppard agreed to pay Kemp $450.00 per year "out of the proceeds of the crop he makes"[85] He agreed to pay Weeks $625.00 with the same terms.[86] Although Carradine's arrangement would have provided him a bonus at the end of year, the terms of Kemp's and Week's contracts imply that if they did not earn at least the amount of their salaries, payment would not be forthcoming.

Sheppard's overseers also showed their investment in the crops by their estimation of whether they could meet his expectations for a good return. D. T. Weeks reported to Sheppard in 1854, "I calculate to have your request complyed [sic] in the 450 [lb.] average I have out about 70 or 75 bags [and] do feel pretty sure that I have not more than one eighth if that picked."[87] Conveying his own hope of a good crop while also being honest about the current state of affairs, Weeks also wrote, "My only fear is we shall have too much rain if we could get a little rain to start the cotton to growing Again it would make as good crop as last year and maybe better for there is no rust to hurt yet."[88] Ultimately, a good crop added currency to Sheppard's wealth and social standing at a cost too steep for Weeks to bear.

NOTES

1. Hammond, *The Cotton Industry*, 93.
2. Ibid. See also, Bonner, "The Plantation Overseer and Southern Nationalism," 1–3. Bonner echoes Hammond's sentiments with respect to overseers lack of care for the land; Bertram Wilbur Doyle, *The Etiquette of Race Relations in the South: A Study in Social Control* (Chicago: University of Chicago Press, 1937), 28. Doyle writes of the overseers' general irascibility and untrustworthiness.
3. Bassett and Polk, *The Southern Plantation Overseer As Revealed in His Letters*, 6.
4. Ibid., p. 7.
5. See Bonner, who wrote against common misconceptions of overseers as untrained in agricultural science. Bonner, "The Plantation Overseer and Southern Nationalism," 1–11.
6. Bonner, "The Plantation Overseer and Southern Nationalism," 1 fn. 5. Emphasis mine. See also Doyle, *The Etiquette of Race Relations in the South*, 32–33. Doyle argues that overseers were kept outside of planters' familial and social circles, and that enslaved men and women were not deferential when overseers attempted to play the part of a planter.
7. Graham v. Roark, 23 Ark. 19, 21 (1861).
8. Ibid., p. 21.
9. Ibid., p. 22.
10. Ibid.
11. Ibid.
12. Ibid., p. 23.
13. Lindsay v. Griffin, 22 Ala 629 (1853).
14. Ibid., p. 629.
15. Ibid.
16. Ibid.
17. Ibid.
18. Ibid.
19. Ibid.
20. Ibid., p. 630.
21. James v. Clarke County, 33 Ala. 51 (1858).
22. Ibid., pp. 51–52.
23. Ibid., p. 51.
24. Ibid.
25. Ibid., p. 52.
26. Ibid., p. 51.
27. Ibid., p. 52.
28. Ibid.
29. Ibid.
30. Porter v. Thomas, 23 Ga. 467 (1857).
31. Ibid., p. 467.
32. Ibid., pp. 467–468.

33. Ibid., p. 468.
34. Ibid.
35. Ibid.
36. Ibid.
37. Ibid., pp. 468–469.
38. Ibid., p. 469.
39. Ibid.
40. Ibid.
41. Ibid.
42. Ibid., p. 471.
43. Ibid., p. 473.
44. Ibid.
45. Scarborough, *The Overseer*, 21–22.
46. Bassett and Polk, *The Southern Plantation Overseer As Revealed in His Letters*, 7.
47. Bonner, "The Plantation Overseer and Southern Nationalism," 1 fn. 5.
48. Scarborough, *The Overseer*, 21–22. As stated in part by this letter of recommendation, "Rec'd a letter from Wm. Hall making enquiry [*sic*] about Mr. Robinson's qualifications as an overseer, In reply I gave Mr. R. credit for honesty, sobriety, and agreeableness."
49. Ibid., p. 105. Such moral requirements were not uncommon. In the words of an Alabaman overseer, Daniel Coleman, which appeared in the periodical the Southern Cultivator: "An overseer should be a moral and sober man, because he should enforce the observance of morality on farm."
50. Letter to Martha J. Jackson from James A. [Tunnavant?], October 1841, JPFP.
51. Overseer Contract between Martha J. Jackson, Henry R. Jackson, and Vincent A. Pierson, 1847, JPFP.
52. Overseer Contract between Martha J. Jackson, Henry R. Jackson, and Vincent A. Pierson, 1847, JPFP. Emphasis mine. Although the language in which these moral requirements are framed might be extreme, the requirements themselves were not uncommon.
53. Overseer Contract between Martha J. Jackson, Henry R. Jackson, and Vincent A. Pierson, 1847, JPFP.
54. Overseer Contract between James Sheppard and Thomas Senoir, January 2, 1847, JSP.
55. Overseer Contract between James Sheppard and Thomas Senoir, January 2, 1847, JSP.
56. Thomas Affleck, "The Duties of An Overseer," in JMJPJ.
57. Ibid.
58. Ibid. For a contrast to overseers' societal roles, see Drew Gilpin Faust's discussion of James Henry Hammond's role in his community. His benevolence and receiving people into his home was part and parcel of a planter's class status. Faust, *James Henry Hammond and the Old South*, 131–134.
59. Letter to Martha J. Jackson from James A. [Tunnavant?], October, 1841, JPFP.

60. Although Faust argues that the same was true for James Henry Hammond and his contemporaries, the significance here is that these standards were implemented contractually and had social implications. See generally Faust, *James Henry Hammond and the Old South*.

61. Overseer Contract between Martha J. Jackson, Henry R. Jackson, and Vincent A. Pierson, 1847, JPFP. Although the argument could be made that Mrs. Jackson's affiliation with the Whig Party made her a temperance advocate, previously presented letters and contract provisions suggest that her politics were not the sole reason for the existence of sobriety standards in the overseer's contract. For an explanation of Whigs and temperance, see Lawrence Frederick Kohl, *The Politics of Individualism: Parties and the American Character in the Jacksonian Era* (New York: Oxford University Press, 1989), 74. See, for example, the overseer's "resume." Letter to Martha J. Jackson from James A. [Tunnavant?], October, 1841, JPFP. There is no evidence that James knew Martha's political leanings, but yet evidence of his sobriety also appears in the letter. The undersigned who attest to his soberness also attest to his other attributes of industriousness and managerial skills. This lends support to my contention that references who attest to teetotalism were not needed only in the letters of those applicants desiring work on the Jackson plantation. See also Scarborough, *The Overseer*, 105.

62. Letter from Wilson Lumpkin to Henry R. Jackson Esq., October 13, 1841, JPFP.

63. Letter from Martha J. Jackson to friend of Henry Jackson (deceased husband) (unnamed), October 10, 1841, JPFP.

64. Letter from Wilson Lumpkin to Henry R. Jackson Esq., October 13, 1841, JPFP. The Wilson Lumpkin mentioned in this letter was likely the Athens, Georgia, planter famous for divesting Georgia land from the Cherokee Nation, and for rising through the political ranks to become a two-term governor of Georgia. See generally Wilson Lumpkin, *The Removal of the Cherokee Indians from Georgia* (New York: Dodd, Mead & Company 1907).

65. Although political office is not the traditional employer/employee relationship, explicit queries into the character and integrity of a potential political candidate would be relevant, no doubt.

66. For example, Faust discusses Hammond's goal to become a part of the world of wealth and influence and his embodiment of a stringent work ethic (instilled in him by his father). Faust, *James Henry Hammond and the Old South*, 26; 8–9. Compare to years later when Hammond had reached his goal. Although both of his male siblings, Marcellus and John, were admitted into the most high ranking educational facilities (West Point and Moses Waddel's school at Willington) neither had the inclination or drive to be there. In Faust's description, "The elder [Marcellus] was boisterous, belligerent, and entirely irresponsible; the younger [John], sullen and lazy. James endeavored to instill in them the ambition and drive his father had imparted to him, but they found it all too easy simply to rely on his social and financial success." Faust, *James Henry Hammond and the Old South*, 146–147. Emphasis mine.

67. Prichard v. Martin, 27 Miss. 305 (1854).

68. Ibid., p. 306.

69. Ibid.
70. Ibid.
71. Ibid., p. 308.
72. Ibid.
73. Ibid.
74. Ibid.
75. Ibid.
76. Ibid.
77. Ibid.
78. Ibid., pp. 311–312.
79. In the words of one disgruntled overseer " If there be . . . a favorable crop year the master makes a splendid crop." Bonner, "The Plantation Overseer and Southern Nationalism," 2.
80. Thomas Affleck, "Duties of an Overseer," in JMJPJ.
81. Overseer Contract between Martha J. Jackson, Henry R. Jackson, and Vincent A. Pierson, 1847, JPFP. Emphasis mine.
82. Letter from Vincent A. Peirson to Martha J. Jackson, July 14, 1844, JPFP. There is no mention as to where Peirson removed the field hands to in the document. He might have removed them from work or to a different place.
83. Letter from Vincent A. Peirson to Martha J. Jackson, September 7, 1844, JPFP.
84. Overseer Contract between James Sheppard and Parker Carradine, January 2, 1840, JSP.
85. Overseers Contract between James Sheppard and Asa Kemp, January 5, 1841, JSP.
86. Overseer Contract between James Sheppard and D. T. Weeks, May 27, 1856, JSP.
87. Letter from D. T. Weeks to James Sheppard, October 1, 1854, JSP.
88. Letter from D. T. Weeks to James Sheppard, August 10, 1854, JSP.

Epilogue
The "Lost Cause" and the Legacy of Plantation Management

In 1858, Thomas Reades Rootes Cobb wrote the first comprehensive book on the law governing enslaved persons, *An Inquiry into the Law of Negro Slavery in the United States of America to Which Is Prefixed an Historical Sketch of Slavery Volume I*.[1] In his writings and musings, this great-nephew of Martha Rootes Cobb Jackson and Henry Jackson, and cousin to Henry Rootes Jackson, their son, was developing what would be key rationales for secession, and arguments for the maintenance of white supremacy.[2] He wrote as a descendant of the planter class,[3] for his family, who owned plantations like Cookshay and Halscot, and employed overseers to work their enslaved labor hard enough to amass and keep their personal wealth. In his words:

> Politically, slavery is a conservative institution. The mass of laborers not being recognized among citizens, every citizen feels that he belongs to an elevated class. It matters not that he is no slaveholder; he is not of the inferior race; he is a freeborn citizen; he engages in no menial occupation. *The poorest meets the richest as an equal; sits at the table with him; salutes him as a neighbor; meets him in every public assembly, and stands on the same social platform.* Hence there is no war of classes. There is truthfully republican equity in the ruling class.[4]

But the ruling class did not include overseers; republican equity did not extend to them. As a White male wage earner in the antebellum south, the overseer's labor was free—he was able to give it to whomever he chose, or keep it for himself—but he was not the planter's equal. He was, however, integral to the maintenance of the plantation economy and preservation of planter wealth. Cotton was king, and although the overseer was not its prince, he was the last line of defense against those increasingly bold citizens of the

Union who would "[rob] the citizens of the Southern States of their property; [inflict] the almost daily occurrence of fugitive slave mobs; and [contribute] to the total insecurity of slave property in the border States."[5] The overseer was the contingency plan for Southern planters ready to go to war to secure their enslaved property and the status they derived from ownership. Later elected as a Georgia representative of the Confederate Congress and an architect of the Confederate Constitution, Cobb would help draft many legislative love letters to the plantocracy that illuminated the "republican equity of the ruling class," and the gross inequities for its managers. Struggles between the Confederate Congress and the Confederate president would decide whether the maintenance of planter wealth was worth the health of the Confederate Republic.

With its ratification of the Confederate Constitution in 1861, the Provisional Confederate Congress provided that "the privilege of the writ of habeas corpus shall not be suspended *unless when in cases of rebellion or invasion the public safety may require it.*"[6] A short time later, the Congressional Congress gave Jefferson Davis, as president of the Confederacy, the authority to suspend the writ, with renewals on that suspension beginning as early as October of 1862.[7] In the context of the Civil War, suspension of the writ meant, in part, that the Confederate military would be able to exercise its control over those living in the Confederate States.[8] Growing tensions between the Confederate Congress and Confederate President, Jefferson Davis, over suspending the writ reached a critical point in February of 1864, when Davis claimed his suspension power was necessary to prevent spies from betraying the Confederacy.[9] The Confederate Congress temporarily restored Davis's suspension powers from February—August 1, 1864, a move roundly disparaged by legislators in the key cotton states—Georgia, Mississippi, and Alabama.[10] Perhaps one planter objection to Jefferson's suspension power was that it interfered with their hired managers, overseers, who caught up in conflicts over the Conscription Act exemptions and its repeal were jailed for failure to serve in the Confederate military.[11] Planters absent from their land and enslaved labor due to military service or otherwise found the basis of their wealth threatened, even as Davis exercised his suspension power to protect their property from an encroaching Union horde.[12]

The Constitution of the Confederate States of America made clear that the primary, enduring purpose of secession was to protect planter's investment in its enslaved labor. Article IV, section 2, part 3 asserts that

> No slave or other person held to service or labor in any State or Territory of the Confederate States, under the laws thereof, escaping or lawfully carried into another, shall, in consequence of any law or regulation therein, be discharged

from such service or labor, but shall be delivered up on claim of the party to whom such slave belongs; or to whom such service or labor may be due.[13]

Two years after its ratification, the Confederate Congress, Cobb among them, drafted a provision exempting overseers from military service. It states in relevant part:

[The] Secretary of War, under the direction of the President, may exempt or detail such other person as he may be satisfied ought to be exempted on account of public necessity, and to insure the production of grain and provisions for the army and the families of soldiers. He may, also, grant exemptions or details, on such terms as he may prescribe, to such overseers, farmers or planters, as he may be satisfied will be more useful to the country in the pursuits of agriculture than in the military service: *Provided,* That such exemptions shall cease whenever the farmer, planter or overseer, shall fail diligently to employ, in good faith, his own skill, capital and labor, exclusively, in the production of grain and provisions, to be sold to the Government and the families of soldiers at prices not exceeding those fixed at the time for like articles by the commissioners of the State under the impressment act.

Although the purpose of the Act on its face seems to be the continued operation of farms to aid the war effort, overseer labor was not needed to manage plantations that were neither large in physical scale, nor plentiful in enslaved labor.[14] The second section of Act emphasized its creators, the public assembly's protection of republican equity in the ruling class. It provided that "[for] the police and management of slaves, there shall be exempted one person on each farm or plantation the sole property of a minor, a person of unsound mind, a feme sole, *or a person absent from home, in the military or naval service of this Confederacy,* on which are *twenty or more slaves.*"[15] The wealthiest planters protected their assets with overseer management as they went off to war, like Thomas Cobb and Henry Jackson, or sent others in their place.[16] For this privilege, planter/enslavers paid $500 into the public treasury.[17] When the Act was repealed just one year later, overseers and their planter/employers litigated overseers' right to manage and receive payment under their employment contracts with planters. They waged battle in the courts, filing writs of habeas corpus, while planter generals and conscripted soldiers lay bloody and broken on the battlefields of a still raging war. The courts with jurisdiction over their contract claims were not the Confederate courts created by a secessionist government.[18] Rather, they were the courts of the Union against which overseer interests in continued employment lay, but upon which their immediate contract interest relied.

James Graham was contractually bound to serve as overseer for Mrs. Eliza E. North through the start of the Civil War.[19] Thirty-seven years old in 1863, Graham was eligible for conscription, which imperiled his management of the fifty-four enslaved men and women on the North plantation.[20] To prevent such an occurrence, Graham and North entered into a contract with the Confederate Conscript Bureau from December 21, 1863 to December 23, 1864, which exempted Graham from military service during that time.[21] Graham qualified for the exemption to the Conscription Act that the Confederate Congress approved on May 1, 1863, because of the fifty-four enslaved laborers that Mrs. North owned, she "[worked] twenty or more hands."[22] For Graham's services and his continued employment under the terms of their contract, Mrs. North paid $500 into the public treasury as required by the terms of the Act.[23] When the Confederate Congress repealed the exemption on February 17, 1864, Graham was arrested and detained, made ready for military service.[24]

Leaving the question of the Confederate government's legitimacy for another day—North and Graham were in a Union court, after all—the court turned its decision-making power to whether it would release Grant's body back to the North plantation.[25] North alleged that the Confederate government had breached its contract with her to allow Graham to continue management of her plantation.[26] She argued that the contract terms for exemption extended a year and were made before the Confederate Congress repealed the exemption provision.[27] Moreover, North had entered into an employment contract with Graham and the Confederate government, both for which she had incurred monetary losses.[28] Of her situation, the court remarked "[the] sense of justice of the dullest mind could not fail to be shocked by an exercise of power, which while the consideration price is retained, would deprive her of her services to which she has thus, in the confidence inspired by the law, purchased a double right."[29] After going through contortionist feats of statutory interpretation to manipulate a just result, the court granted Graham's writ of habeas corpus.[30] His body thus rendered up for service to the plantocracy, Graham was free to manage those enslaved laborers who remained bound.

The Supreme Court of Alabama, a court charged with interpreting the law of its Confederate government,[31] also considered petitions for two writs of habeas corpus for overseers in June of 1864.[32] Captain N. R. H. Dawson had detained William L. Strawbridge and William C. Mays for service in his militia over the objections of their deceased planters' executor, William H. Fellows.[33] Prior to their arrests, Fellows hired Mays to work as an overseer on the Childers plantation, and Strawbridge to work as an overseer on the Strawbridge plantation.[34] Each plantation had upward of fifteen enslaved laborers and both overseers were employed to manage those laborers beginning in January of 1864.[35]

Problems arose in May 1864 when Fellows applied for Mays and Strawbridge to be exempt from military service.[36] Although both men met the overseer exemption requirements as set out in the May 1863 Act, the Confederate Congress approved another act on February 17, 1864, "to organize forces to serve during the war."[37] The terms of the act provided

> that from and after the passage of this act, *all white men, residents of the Confederate States*, between the ages of seventeen and fifty, shall be in the military service of the Confederate States for the war.
> SEC. 2. That all the persons aforesaid, between the ages of eighteen and forty-five, *now in service*, shall be retained, during the present war with the United States, *in the same regiments, battalions and companies to which they belong at the passage of this act, with the same organization and officers, unless regularly transferred or discharged, in accordance with the laws and regulations for the government of the army.*[38]

Because Mays and Strawbridge had been enrolled in the Confederate draft prior to Fellows's application and the passage of the February 1864 Act, they were required by its provisions to remain in military service even though they had not formally served.[39] The trial court granted both men's habeas petitions and ordered them released to their respective plantations. The State of Alabama, on behalf of the Confederate government and its military, appealed.[40]

On appeal, the court framed the issue before it as "does the State law [governing enrollment into the Confederate military, which exempts] 'overseers,' relate to and embrace only the acts of the Confederate Congress then in existence; or does it also relate to and include acts or laws of the Confederate States which might be subsequently enacted, exempting *overseers*."[41] In considering its question, the court first clarified the law at issue. At the time of Fellows's application, the overseer exemption enacted on May 1, 1863, had been repealed with respect to the requirement that overseers seeking exemption manage at least twenty enslaved persons.[42] However, it had not been repealed as to overseer exemption altogether. The revised provision exempted overseers who had (1) managed at least fifteen enslaved plantation or farm laborers age sixteen-fifty since January 1, 1864; and (2) worked on a plantation or farm where all of the White males were eligible for the draft.[43] To confer the favor of exemption, the Confederate government exacted a payment in 100 lbs. of bacon, equal amounts of pork, or beef, for which it would pay the government rate as rations for its soldiers.[44]

The court discussed the conflict brought about by exempting overseers of the wealthiest planters, at the expense of small-scale farmers who could not afford overseers, and had few options to manage their farms in their absence.[45] In a series of dueling opinions, it debated whether overseers were best utilized serving the interests of the plantocracy or the Confederacy, as it sacrificed ever more bodies to preserve its "way of life." Justice Walker deemed it "inexorable" that the Confederate government would make overseers untouchable with respect to state military service, and decried planter economic self-interests in supplying commodities for the war effort.[46] Justice Stone argued that overseer skill in managing the agricultural interests of the state was equally important to the war, as their actions led directly to feeding Confederate soldiers and their families.[47] He reasoned "[the acts exempting overseers from military service] prove, that the control and profitable employment of the slave-labor of the country were the objects of the enactment; and that this labor should be made tributary to the prosecution of the giant war to which we are now engaged."[48] Through these multiple lenses, the court, in an opinion delivered by Justice Phelan, determined that the trial court dismissed Mays and Strawbridge from state military service, but did not dismiss them from their military obligations to the Confederate States of America.[49] Thus, the Alabama law governing conscription did "relate to and include acts or laws of the Confederate States which might be subsequently enacted, exempting *overseers*." Had Mays and Strawbridge not enrolled as conscripts, thus placing themselves within the control of the Confederate government, their exemption would stand. However, their occupation would have greatly diminished.[50] In the court's words:

> [there] need be no such great alarm about the *supervision of the labor* of the country. If the holy cause of liberty requires it, many more farms and plantations can be pretty well managed, as thousands now are, where their brave owners have either lain down their lives, or stand ready to do so in the ranks of their country, *without the supervision of able-bodied men. The heroic women, with their barefooted boys and girls, the old men, the convalescent or disabled soldiers, and though last, by no means least, the experienced and faithful negro, will do the business.* The want of subsistence, from the beginning of this gigantic struggle for all that men hold dear, up to this time, though sometimes, and in some places, pressing, has never been half so pressing as the want of able-bodied men to recruit the ranks of our noble and devoted armies.[51]

And just like that, the court made overseers obsolete. Overseers, "[the] class of men who have the management of slaves on the plantation or elsewhere, as the agent or employee of the owner [and distinct from] the class of owners," would fight to preserve that most unequal distinction as the Civil War hurdled toward its end.[52] They would go off to die in a cause that was not lost but only hiding until overseers could be remade as modern managers and the cause of their employers could take its next pernicious form.

In the present day, the managerial position of "overseer" that White men defined through myriad legal, contractual, and daily social and professional negotiations evokes the fear of violence, surveillance, and degradation. Black employees in employment discrimination lawsuits have described their workplaces as modern-day plantations,[53] with managers acting as overseers, watching and waiting for opportunities to mete out punishment for their "slacking off."[54] The legal record contains harrowing examples of modern-day managers and coworkers referring to themselves or being introduced by other managers or coworkers as overseers to Black employees,[55] and even going so far as to snap a whip to urge a Black employee to work.[56] That this imagery is employed to harass and subdue should give us pause, especially as it is backed with the managerial authority to negatively impact the lives of Black employees in any employment context throughout the United States. This is the troubling legacy of plantation management—the deep imprint of White masculinities on the managerial identity that pervades our workplaces in the modern world.

NOTES

1. Thomas Reade Rootes Cobb, *An Inquiry into the Law of Negro Slavery in the United States of America to which Is Prefixed an Historical Sketch of Slavery Volume I* (Savannah: W. Thorne Williams, 1858).

2. Kenneth Coleman, *Athens 1861–1865, as Seen Through Letters in the University of Georgia Libraries* (Athens, University of Georgia Press, 1969), 3–6.

3. Colyer Meriwether, ed., *Publications of the Southern History Association, Volume 11* (Washington, DC: Southern History Association, 1907), 148. "Thomas Reade Rootes Cobb was born in Jefferson County, Georgia, April 10, 1823. While yet a child his father moved to Athens, Georgia. Being a man of very considerable wealth, owner of productive plantations and many slaves, his family lived in luxury and were denied no good thing." Meriwether, *Publications of the Southern History Association, Volume 11*, 148. Thomas went on to study at the University of Georgia. By the time he graduated, his father has lost his fortune to debt. Not to be deterred, he studied law, passed the bar exam, and married Marion Lumpkin, daughter to Chief Justice Joseph Henry Lumpkin, first Chief Justice of the Georgia Supreme Court. Meriwether, *Publications of the Southern History Association, Volume 11*, 149–150.

4. Cobb, *An Inquiry into the Law of Negro Slavery*, ccxiii. Emphasis mine.

5. E. N. Elliott, *Cotton is King*, iv–v.

6. *The Constitution of the Confederate States of America*, Article I §9, 3 (1861); See generally Wilfred Buck Yearns, *The Confederate Congress* (Athens: University of Georgia Press, 1960).

7. G. Edward White, *Recovering the Legal History of the Confederacy*, 68 Wash. & Lee L. Rev. 467, 535 (2011).

8. White, *Recovering the Legal History of the Confederacy*, 536–537.

9. Ibid., p. 537.

10. Ibid.

11. Ibid., p. 539.

12. Ibid., pp. 537–538.

13. *The Constitution of the Confederate States of America*, Article IV §2, cl. 3. See also Article IV, §3, cl. 3: "The Confederate States may acquire new territory; and Congress shall have the power to legislate and provide governments for the inhabitants of all territory belonging to the Confederate States, lying without the limits of the several States; and may permit them, at such times and in such manner as it may by law provide, to form States to be admitted into the Confederacy. In all such territory the institution of negro slavery, as it now exists in the Confederate States, shall be recognized and protected by Congress and by the Territorial government; and the inhabitants of the several Confederate States and Territories shall have the right to take such Territory any slaves lawfully held by them in any of the States or Territories of the Confederate States."

14. Albert Burton Moore, *Conscription and Conflict in the Confederacy* (New York: The Macmillan Company, 1924), 64–65. Moore discusses the widening of conscription exemptions to include overseers. He explains, "[the] planters, especially, felt that their plantations, which were of prime importance to the sustenance of the army and the public, had received scant consideration at the hands of Congress; and they launched a propaganda early in the [spring of 1862] to secure equality with the industrial groups before the law. An effort was made to have persons who had been enrolled detailed as overseers, but the Secretary of War refused them relief and suggested that they should carry their case before Congress in August [1862]. It was reported that Governor Moore of Louisiana uniformly ordered his colonels to leave one white man on every plantation, but the President informed Governor Pettus of Mississippi that there was no authority under the existing law to exempt overseers. By persistent effort they established their cause before Congress and were given relief by the exemption act of October 11th [1862]." Moore, *Conscription and Conflict in the Confederacy*, 64–65. The Act was approved on May 1, 1863, which repealed the October 11, 1862, provision for twenty or more slaves. *The Statutes at Large of the Confederate States of America*, Chapter LXXX §§ 1 & 2 (1863). See also White, *Recovering the Legal History of the Confederacy*, 545–546. Of the Act, White states, "On its face, the exemption was an apparent effort to favor planters over farmers who owned no slaves. The exemption's 'influence upon the poor,' one member of Congress wrote to [Jefferson] Davis in December 1862, 'is most calamitous, and has awakened a spirit and elicited a discussion of which we may safely predicate the most unfortunate results.' "

15. Ex parte Graham, 13 Rich 277, 279 (1864). Emphasis mine.

16. Thomas Cobb is best known for organizing Cobb's Legion, a military battalion that served in the Civil War. Cobb's official title was "Brigadier-General." Harriet Bey Mesic, *Cobb's Legion Calvary: A History and Roster of the Ninth Georgia Volunteers in the Civil War* (Jefferson: McFarland & Company, Inc., 2011). Henry Rootes Jackson also served in many military regiments throughout the Civil War. See Ezra J. Warner, *Generals in Grey: Lives of the Confederate Commanders* (Baton Rouge: Louisiana State University Press, 2002), 72; John E. Eicher and David J. Eicher, *Civil War High Commands* (Stanford: Stanford University Press, 2001),

178, 876, 889. For more on the practice of substitution, see Moore, *Conscription and Conflict in the Confederacy*, 28–29. Moore writes of substitution "[although] the chief purpose of substitution was to utilize the potentialities of men along industrial lines, there was from the beginning, as might have been expected, a general propensity to regard it through purely private considerations . . . . Some of those who had wealth and could not secure immunity under the exemption act made a rush for substitutes, and in their anxiety to procure them were not very scrupulous about complying with the law."

17. Ex parte Graham, 13 Rich at 279 (1864).
18. For more on Confederate Courts, see White, *Recovering the Legal History of the Confederacy*, 509–529.
19. Ex parte Graham, 13 Rich at 279, 282, 285 (1864).
20. Ibid., p. 277.
21. Ibid., pp. 277–278.
22. Ibid., pp. 277–278; 282.
23. Ibid., p. 278.
24. Ibid., pp. 278, 282.
25. Ibid., p. 283.
26. Ibid., p. 283.
27. Ibid., pp. 282–283.
28. Ibid., p. 285.
29. Ibid., p. 285.
30. Ibid., p. 290.
31. In re Strawbridge, 39 Ala. 367, 379 (1864). The court agreed to the argument that "[the] Constitution of the Confederate States, and laws made in pursuance thereof, are the supreme law of the land; and if the laws of the state, and those of the Confederate States aforesaid, come in conflict, the former as the paramount law, must prevail."
32. Ibid., p. 367.
33. Ibid., p. 367.
34. Ibid., pp. 367–368.
35. Ibid., pp. 367–368.
36. Ibid., pp. 368–369.
37. *The Statutes at Large of the Confederate States of America*, Chapter LXV (1864).
38. Ibid. Emphasis mine.
39. In re Strawbridge, 39 Ala. at 369–70.
40. Ibid., p. 369.
41. Ibid., p. 370. Emphasis in the original.
42. Ibid., p. 372.
43. Ibid., p. 372.
44. Ibid., p. 372–373.
45. Ibid., p. 378–379.
46. Ibid., p. 388–389.
47. Ibid., p. 403.

48. Ibid., p. 403.
49. Ibid., p. 384–385.
50. Ibid., pp. 384-85.
51. Ibid., p. 384.
52. Ibid., pp. 374–375.

53. For example, *Tillery v. New York State Office of Alcoholism and Substance Abuse Servs.*, No. 1:13-CV-1528, 2010 WL 2870502, at *7 (N.D. New York July 5, 2017). (Black female employee described the workplace as "still structured like . . . a slave plantation with [the manager] acting as overseer.")

54. For example, *Shelby v. American Colloid Co., Inc.*, No. 2:04CV489-T, 2005 WL 3804725, at *4 (M.D. Alabama March 1, 2005). (Black male employee stated the manager "sits up there and watch us like an overseer watching over slaves, smoking, you know. And that kind of gets to us, you know. We don't need that. We know our jobs.")

55. For example, *Pena v. USX Corp.*, No. 2:03CV334, 2006 WL 623595, at *4-5 (N.D. Indiana March 9, 2006). (White male coworker referred to himself as a "slave overseer."); Harvey v. Office of Banks and Real Estate, 377 F. 698, 702–703 (7th Cir. 2004). (White female manager introduced a White male manager to Black employees as their "overseer.")

56. For example, *Johnson v. Potter*, 177 F. Supp. 2d. 961, 964 (D. Minnesota 2001). (White male manager "snapped" a bullwhip at the only black employee, a Black male, and then said, "Let's go to work.")

Bibliography

SECONDARY SOURCES

Books

Affleck, Thomas. *The Cotton Plantation Record and Account Book No. 1, Suitable for a Force of 40 Hands or Under.* New Orleans: B.M. Norman, 1847.

Allen, Theodore W. *The Invention of the White Race, Volume One: Racial Oppression and Social Control.* New York: Verso, 2000.

Bancroft, Frederic. *Slave Trading in the Old South.* New York: Frederick Ungar Publishing, 1959.

Baptist, Edward E. *The Half Has Never Been Told: Slavery and the Making of American Capitalism.* New York: Basic Books, 2014.

Bassett, John Spencer, John Spencer and Polk, James Knox. *The Southern Plantation Overseer As Revealed in His Letters.* Northampton: Smith College, 1925.

Beckert, Sven. *Empire of Cotton: A Global History.* New York: Vintage Books 2014.

Blackstone, Sir William. *Commentaries on the Laws of England in Four Books, Book 1.* London: Banks & Brothers, 1893.

Bolton, Charles C. *Poor Whites of the Antebellum South: Tenants and Laborers in Central North Carolina and Northeast Mississippi.* Durham: Duke University Press, 1994.

Breeden, James O ed. *Advice Among Masters: The Ideal In Slave Management in the Old South.* Connecticut: Greenwood Press, 1980.

Bruchey, Stuart Weems *Cotton and the Growth of the American Economy: 1790–1860: Sources and Readings.* New York: Harcourt, Brace & World, 1967.

Burton, Orville Vernon and Robert C. McMath eds. *Class, Conflict, and Consensus: Antebellum Southern Community Studies.* Connecticut: Greenwood Press, 1982.

Chandler, Alfred D. Jr. *The Visible Hand: The Managerial Revolution in American Business.* Cambridge: Harvard University Press, 1977.

Chaplin, Joyce E. *An Anxious Pursuit: Agricultural Innovation and Modernity in the Lower South, 1730–1815.* Chapel Hill: University of North Carolina Press, 1993.

Clark, Christine and O'Donnell, James, eds., *Becoming and Unbecoming White: Owning and Disowning a Racial Identity.* Westport: Praeger Publishers, 1999.

Cobb, Thomas Reade Rootes. *An Inquiry into the Law of Negro Slavery in the United States of America to which is prefixed An Historical Sketch of Slavery Volume I.* Savannah: W. Thorne Williams: 1858.

Coleman, Kenneth. *Athens 1861–1865, as Seen Through Letters in the University of Georgia Libraries.* Athens, University of Georgia Press, 1969.

Collins, Hugh, *Regulating Contracts.* Oxford: Oxford University Press, 1999.

Collins, Patricia Hill. Black Feminist Thought: Knowledge, Consciousness, and the Politics of Empowerment. New York: Routledge, 2000.

Coulter, E. Merton. *Daniel Lee: Agriculturalist: His Life North and South.* Athens: University of Georgia Press, 1972.

Davis, Jefferson. *The Papers of Jefferson Davis: 1856–1860*, eds., Mary Seaton Dix, Lynda Lasswell Crist. Baton Rouge: Louisiana State University Press, 1989.

Doyle, Bertram Wilbur, *The Etiquette of Race Relations in the South, A Study in Social Control.* Chicago: University of Chicago Press, 1937.

Durocher, Kristina. *Raising Racists: The Socialization of White Children in the Jim Crow South.* Lexington: The University Press of Kentucky, 2011.

Eicher, John E. and Eicher, David J. *Civil War High Commands.* Stanford: Stanford University Press, 2001.

Elliott, E.N. ed., *Cotton is King and Pro-Slavery Arguments Comprising the Writings of Hammond, Harper, Christy, Stringfellow, Hodge, Bledsoe, and Cartwright.* Augusta: Pritchard, Abbott & Loomis, 1860.

Faust, Drew Gilpin. *James Henry Hammond and the Old South: A Design for Mastery*, Baton Rouge: Louisiana State University Press, 1982.

Ford, Lacy K. Jr. *Origins of Southern Radicalism: The South Carolina Upcountry, 1800–1860.* New York: Oxford University Press, 1988.

Foster, William O. Sr., *James Jackson: Duelist and Militant Statesman 1757–1806.* Athens: University of Georgia Press, 2009.

Fredrickson, George M. *The Black Image in the White Mind.* New York: Harper & Roe, 1971.

Genovese, Eugene D. *Roll Jordon Roll: The World The Slaves Made.* New York, Vintage Books, 1972.

Genovese, Eugene and Fox-Genovese, Elizabeth, *Fatal Self-Deception: Slaveholding Paternalism in the Old South.* New York: Cambridge University Press, 2011.

Gilmore, Grant. *Security Interests in Personal Property.* Boston: Little Brown, 1965.

Gray, Lewis Cecil. *History of Agriculture in the Southern United States to 1860: Volume I.* Baltimore: Waverly Press Inc., 1933.

Gray, Lewis Cecil. *History of Agriculture in the Southern United States to 1860: Volume II.* Baltimore: Waverly Press Inc., 1933.

Gross, Ariela J. *Double Character: Slavery and Mastery in the Antebellum Southern Courtroom.* Princeton: Princeton University Press, 2000.

Hahn, Steven. *The Roots of Southern Populism: Yeoman Farmers and the Transformation of the Georgia Upcountry 1850–1890.* New York: Oxford University Press, 1983.

Hammond, M.B. *The Cotton Industry Part I: The Cotton Culture and the Cotton Trade.* New York: The Macmillan Company, 1897.

Harris, J. William. *Plain Folk and Gentry: White Identity and Black Slavery in Augusta's Hinterlands.* Baton Rouge: Louisiana State University Press, 1987.

Helms, Janet E. *Black and White Racial Identity: Theory, Research and Practice.* Westport: Praeger Publishers, 1990.

Hooks, Bell. *Feminism is for Everybody: Passionate Politics.* London: Pluto Press, 2000.

Hughey, Matthew E. *White Bound: Nationalists, Antiracists and the Shared Meanings of Race.* Stanford: Stanford University Press, 2012.

Jackson II, Ronald L. *The Negotiation of Cultural Identity: Perceptions of European American. and African Americans.* Westport: Praeger Publishers, 1999.

Johnson, Walter *River of Dark Dreams: Slavery and Empire in the Cotton Kingdom.* Cambridge: Harvard University Press, 2013.

Jones-Rogers, Stephanie E. *They Were Her Property: White Woman As Slave Owners in the American South.* New Haven: Yale University Press, 2019.

Kohl, Lawrence Frederick. *The Politics of Individualism: Parties and the American Character in the Jacksonian Era.* New York: Oxford University Press, 1989.

Kimmel, Michael. *Manhood in America: A Cultural History.* New York: Oxford University Press, 2006.

Lipsitz, George. *The Possessive Investment in Whiteness: How White People Profit from Identity Politics.* Philadelphia: Temple University Press, 2006.

Lumley, Frederick Elmore. *Means of Social Control.* New York: The Century, 1925.

Lumpkin, Wilson. *The Removal of the Cherokee Indians from Georgia.* New York: Dodd, Mead & Company 1907.

Magdol, Edward and Wakelyn, Jon L. *The Southern Common People: Studies in Nineteenth Century Social History.* Westport: Greenwood Press, 1980.

Majewski, Modernizing. *A Slave Economy: The Economic Vision of the Confederate Nation.* Chapel Hill: University of North Carolina Press, 2009.

Meriwether, Colyer ed., *Publications of the Southern History Association, Volume 11.* Washington, DC: Southern History Association, 1907.

Merritt, Keri Leigh. *Masterless Men: Poor Whites and Slavery in the Antebellum South.* New York: Cambridge University Press, 2017.

Mesic, Harriet Bey. *Cobb's Legion Calvary: A History and Roster of the Ninth Georgia Volunteers in the Civil War.* Jefferson: McFarland & Company, Inc., 2011.

McCurry, Stephanie. *Masters of Small Worlds: Yeoman Households, Gender Relations, and the Political Culture of the Antebellum South Carolina Low Country.* New York: Oxford University Press, 1995.

Moore, Albert Burton. *Conscription and Conflict in the Confederacy.* New York: The Macmillan Company, 1924.

Morris, Thomas D., *Southern Slavery and the Law, 1619–1860.* Chapel Hill: University of North Carolina Press, 1996.

Northup, Solomon. *Twelve Years A Slave*. 2009. Kindle.
Oakes, James. *The Ruling Race: A History of American Slaveholders*. New York: W.W. Norton & Company, 1998.
Olmsted, Frederick Law. *The Cotton Kingdom: A Traveller's Observations on Cotton and Slavery in the American Slave States, 1853–1861*. 2017. Kindle.
Otto, John Solomon. *Cannon's Point Plantation 1794–1860: Living Conditions and Status Patterns in the Old South*. Orlando: Academic Press, 1984.
Phillips, Ulrich B. *American Negro Slavery*. New York: D. Appleton Century Company Inc., 1933.
Phillips, Ulrich B. *The Course of the South to Secession*. D. Appleton Century Company Inc., 1939.
Powell, John Joseph. *Essay Upon the Law of Contracts and Agreements*. London: J. Johnson and T. Whieldon, 1790.
Ritterhouse, Jennifer. *Growing Up Jim Crow: How Black and White Southern Children Learned Race*. Chapel Hill: University of North Carolina Press, 2006.
Robbins, Stephens P. *Management*. Upper Saddle River: Prentice Hall, 1994.
Rockman, Seth. *Scraping By: Wage Labor, Slavery, and Survival in Early Baltimore*. Baltimore: Johns Hopkins University Press, 2009.
Roediger, David R. *The Wages of Whiteness: Race and The Making of the American Working Class*. New York: Verso, 1991.
Roediger, David R. ed., *Colored White: Transcending the Racial Past*. Berkeley: University of California Press, 2002.
Rosenthal, Caitlin. *Accounting for Slavery: Masters and Management*. Cambridge: Harvard University Press, 2018.
Scarborough, William Kauffman. *The Overseer: Plantation Management in the Old South*. Louisiana: Louisiana State University Press, 1966.
Shermerhorn, Calvin. *The Business of Slavery and the Rise of American Capitalism*. New Haven: Yale University Press, 2015.
Stubbs, Tristan, *Masters of Violence: The Plantation Overseers of Eighteenth-Century Virginia, South Carolina, and Georgia*. Columbia: University of South Carolina Press, 2018.
Thomas, E. *A Concise View of the Slavery of the People of Color in the United States*. Philadelphia: E. Thomas, 1834.
Van Deburg, William L. *The Slave Drivers: Black Agricultural Labor Supervisors in the Antebellum South*. New York: Oxford University Press, 1979.
Warner, Ezra J. *Generals in Grey: Lives of the Confederate Commanders*. Baton Rouge: Louisiana State University Press, 2002.
White, G. Edward. *Recovering the Legal History of the Confederacy*, 68 Wash. & Lee L. Rev. 467, 2011.
Wiethoff, William E. *Crafting the Overseer's Image*. Columbia: University of South Carolina Press, 2006.
Wood, Kirsten E. *Masterful Women: Slaveholding Widows from the American Revolution through the Civil War*. Chapel Hill: University of North Carolina Press, 2004.

Woodward, Kath ed., *Questioning Identity: Gender, Class, Ethnicity.* New York: Routledge, 2004.
Wright, Gavin. *The Political Economy of the South: Households, Markets, and Wealth in the Nineteenth Century.* New York: W.W. Norton & Company Inc., 1978.
Wyatt-Brown, Bertram, *Honor and Violence in the Old South.* New York: Oxford University Press, 1986.
Yearns, Wilfred Buck. *The Confederate Congress.* Athens: University of Georgia Press, 1960.

Book Chapters

Campbell, Hugh, Bell, Michael Mayerfeld and Finney, Margaret. "Masculinity and Rural Life: An Introduction," In *Country Boys: Masculinity and Rural Life*, edited by Hugh Campbell, Michael, Mayerfeld Bell and Margaret Finney, 1–22. University Park, The Pennsylvania State University Press, 2006.
Fields, Barbara J. "Ideology and Race in American History," In *Region, Race, and Reconstruction: Essays in Honor of C. Vann Woodward*, edited by J. Morgan Kousser and James M. McPherson, 143–177. New York: Oxford University Press, 1982.
Hahn, Steven. "The Yeomanry in the Non-Plantation South: Upper Piedmont Georgia, 1850–1860." *Class, Conflict, and Consensus: Antebellum Southern Community Studies*, edited by Orville Vernon Burton and Robert C. McMath, 29–56. Connecticut: Greenwood Press, 1982.
Otto, John Solomon. "Race and Class on Antebellum Plantations" In *Archaeological Perspectives on Ethnicity in America: Afro-American and Asian American Culture History,* edited by Robert L. Schuyler, 3–13. Amityville: Baywood Publishing, 1980.
Rosenthal, Caitlin. "Slavery's Scientific Management: Masters and Managers," In *Slavery's Capitalism: A New History of American Economic Development*, edited by Sven Beckert, 62–86. Philadelphia: University of Pennsylvania Press, 2016.

Dissertations, Theses, and Papers

Boodry, Kathryn Susan, "The Common Thread: Slavery, Cotton, and Atlantic Finance from the Louisiana Purchase to Reconstruction." PhD diss., Harvard University, 2014.
Westfield, Kelly "The Enslaved Members of the Davenport Household: Geography, Mobility, and Pre-Davenport House Lived Experiences," MA Thesis, Georgia Southern University, 2018.

Articles

Barnett, Randy. *A Consent Theory of Contract*, 86 Colum. L. Rev. 269 (1986).
Bonner, James Calvin. "The Plantation Overseer and Southern Nationalism as Revealed in the Career of Garland D. Harmon." *Agricultural History*, 19 (January 1945): 1–11.

Christian, Schuyler Medlock. "A Sketch of the History of Science in Georgia." *The Georgia Review* 2, no. 4 (Winter 1948): 415–427.

Dowd, Nancy E. *Masculinities and Feminist Legal Theory*, 23 Wisc. J.L. Gender & Soc'y 201 (2008).

Connell, R.W., R. W. and Messerschmidt, James. "Hegemonic Masculinity: Rethinking the Concept." *Gender & Society* 19, no. 6 (December 2005): 829–859.

Conrad, Alfred H. and Meyer, John R. "The Economics of Slavery in the Antebellum South." *Journal of Political Economy*, 66, no. 2 (April 1958): 95–130.

Cooke, Bill "The Denial of Slavery in Management Studies." *Journal of Management Studies*, 40, no. 8 (December 2003): 1895–1918.

Depuydt, Peter. "The Mortgaging of Souls: Sugar, Slaves, and Speculation." *Louisiana History: Journal of the Louisiana History Association* 54, no. 4 (Fall 2013): 448–464.

Foust, James D. and Swan, Dale E. "Productivity and Profitability of Antebellum Slave Labor: A Micro-Approach." *Agricultural History*, 44, no. 1 (January 1970): 39–62.

Gold, Andrew S. *A Property Theory of Contract*, 103 Nw. U. L. Rev. 1 (2009).

Gross, Ariela. *"Like Master, Like Man": Constructing Whiteness in the Commercial Law of Slavery, 1800–1861*, 18 Cardozo L. Rev. 263 (1996).

Heier, Jan Richard. "A Content Comparison of Antebellum Plantation Records and Thomas Affleck's Accounting Principles." *The Accounting Historians Journal* 15, no. 2 (Fall 1988): 131–150.

Horowitz, Morton J. *The Historical Foundations of Modern Contract Law*, 87 Harv. L. Rev. 917 1974).

Kuruvila, Bikku. *Financialization, Inequality, Stagnation, and Vulnerability in Historical Perspective: Foregrounding the Human Impact of State Policy and the Law from the U.S. to India*, 22 Trinity La. Rev. 1 (2016).

Lawrence, Alexander A. "James Jackson: Passionate Patriot," *The Georgia Historical Quarterly* 34, no. 2 (June 1950): 75–86.

Lebergott, Stanley. "The Demand for Land, The United States, 1820–1860." *The Journal of Economic History* 45, no. 2 (June 1985): 181–212.

Martin, Bonnie. "Slavery's Invisible Engine: Mortgaging Human Property." *Journal of Southern History* 76, no. 4 (November 2010): 817–866.

Olmstead, Alan L. and Rhode, Paul W. "Cotton, Slavery, and the New History of Capitalism." *Explorations in Economic History* 67 (January 2018): 1–17.

Phillips, Ulrich B. "The Central Theme of Southern History." *American Historical Review* 34, no. 1 (October 1928): 30–43.

Scarborough, William Kauffman. "The Southern Plantation Overseer: A Re-Evaluation." *Agricultural History* 38 (January 1964): 13–20.

Stafford, L. Scott. *Slavery and the Arkansas Supreme Court*, 19 U. Ark. Little Rock L.J. 413 (1997).

Sutch, Richard. "The Profitability of Antebellum Slavery: Revisited." *Southern Economic Journal* 31, no. 4 (April 1965): 365–377.

Vandervelde, Lea. *The Last Legally Beaten Servant in America: From Compulsion to Coercion in the American Workplace*, 39 Seattle U.L. Rev. 727 (2016).

Wahl, Jenny Bourne. *Legal Contraints on Slave Masters: The Problem of Social Cost*, 41 Am. J. Legal Hist. 1 (1997).
Weitzman, Martin L. "'The Ratchet Principle'" and Performance Incentives." *The Bell Journal of Economics* 11, no. 1 (Spring 1980): 302–308.

PRIMARY SOURCES

Archival Collections

Haller Nutt Papers, (1846–1860) and Journal of "Araby" Plantation 1843–1850. In *Records of Ante-Bellum Southern Plantations from the Revolution to the Civil War*, gen.ed. Kenneth Stampp, Series F, Pt. 1. Frederick, Maryland: University Publications of America, c1985. (abbreviated as HNP-JAP)

Jackson and Prince Family Papers, 1784–1880. In *Records of Ante-Bellum Southern Plantations from the Revolution to the Civil War*, gen.ed. Kenneth Stampp, Series J, Part 4. Frederick, Maryland: University Publications of America, c1985. (abbreviated as JPFP)

James Sheppard Papers, 1830–1889. In *Records of Ante-Bellum Southern Plantations from the Revolution to the Civil War*, gen.ed. Kenneth Stampp, Series F, Pt. 1. Frederick, Maryland: UniversityPublications of America, c1985. (abbreviated as JSP)

Joseph M. Jaynes Plantation Journals, 1854–1860. In *Records of Ante-Bellum Southern Plantations from the Revolution to the Civil Wa*r, gen.ed. Kenneth Stampp, Series F, Pt. 1. Frederick, Maryland: University Publications of America, c1985. (abbreviated as JMJPJ)

Samuel O. Wood Papers, 1847–1865. In *Records of Ante-Bellum Southern Plantations from the Revolution to the Civil War*, gen.ed. Kenneth Stampp, Series F, Pt. 1. Frederick, Maryland: University Publications of America, c1985. (abbreviated as SOWP)

Cases

Alfred v. State, 8 George 296 (1859)
Brunson v. Martin, 17 Ark. 270 (1856)
Cox v. State, 32 Ga. 515 (1861)
Cresap v. Winter, 14 La. 553 (1840)
Dowling v. State, 13 Miss. 664 (1846)
Dupre v. Prescott, 5 La.Ann. 592 (1850)
Dwyer v. Cane, 5 La. Ann. 707 (1851)
Garcia v. Garcia, 7 La. Ann. 525 (1852)
Gillian v. Senter, 9 Ala. 395 (1846)
Ex parte Graham, 13 Rich 277, 279 (1864).
Graham v. Roark, 23 Ark. 19 (1861)

Harmon v. Fleming, 25 Miss. 135 (1852)
Harvey v. Office of Banks and Real Estate, 377 F. 698 (7th Cir. 2004)
Hendricks v. Phillips, 3 La. Ann. 618 (1848)
James v. Clarke County, 33 Ala. 51 (1858)
Jacob v. Ursuline Nuns, 2 Mart. (o.s.) 269 (1812)
Johnson v. Lovett, 31 Ga. 187 (1860)
Johnson v. Potter, 177 F. Supp. 2d. 961 (D. Minnesota 2001)
Jordan v. State, 22 Ga. 545 (1857)
Kennedy v. Mason, 10 La. Ann. 519 (1855)
Lambert v. King, 12 La. Ann. 662 (1856)
Lindsay v. Griffin, 22 Ala 629 (1853)
Lynch v. McRee, 18 La.Ann 640 (1866)
Martineau v. Hooper, 8 Mart. (o.s.) 699 (1820)
Miller v. Stewart, 12 La.Ann. 170 (1857)
Molett v. State, 33 Ala. 408 (1859)
Nelson v. Botts, 16 L.A. 596 (1841)
Peake v. Scaife, 11 Rich. 672 (1858)
Pena v. USX Corp., No. 2:03CV334, 2006 WL 623595 (N.D. Indiana March 9, 2006)
Pettigrew v. Bishop, 3 Ala. 440 (1842)
Prichard v. Martin, 27 Miss. 305 (1854)
Porter v. Thomas, 23 Ga. 467 (1857)
Richardson v. Pumphrey, 2 La. Ann. 448 (1847)
Roberts v. Brownrigg, 9 Ala. 106 (1846)
Shelby v. American Colloid Co., Inc., No. 2:04CV489-T, 2005 WL 3804725 (M.D. Alabama March 1, 2005)
In re Strawbridge, 39 Ala. 367 (1864).
State v. Abram, 10 Ala. 928 (1847)
State v. Flanigin, 5 Ala. 477 (1843)
Taylor v. Paterson, 9 La. Ann. 251 (1854)
Thompson v. Bertrand, 23 Ark, 730 (1861)
Tillery v. New York State Office of Alcoholism and Substance Abuse Servs., No. 1:13-CV-1528, 2010 WL 2870502 (N.D. New York July 5, 2017)
Whitley v. Murray, 34 Ala. 155 (1859)
Womack v. Nicholson, 3 Rib (LA) 248 (1842)

Statutes

Alabama Legislative Acts (1847–1848)
Alabama Legislative Acts (1848)
Alabama Slave Code (1852)
Alabama Slave Code (1848)
Alabama Session Law (1855–1856)
Code of Arkansas (1858)
Code of Arkansas (1861)
Code of the State of Georgia (1831)

Laws of Mississippi (1798–1849)
Laws of Mississippi (1823)
Laws of Mississippi, (1840)
Laws of Mississippi (1857)
The Constitution of the Confederate States of America (1861)
The Statutes at Large of the Confederate States of America, Chapter LXXX §§ 1 & 2 (1863)
The Statutes at Large of the Confederate States of America, Chapter LXV (1864)

Index

acre, 15, 17–18, 23, 25, 31, 33, 66
autopsy, 75

bruise, 40. *See* punishment

capitalism, ix, xiii, xvi–xvii, 1, 4, 7, 10, 12, 31, 34, 46, 54, 62, 107, 110–112; account, 3, 18, 23, 26–28, 37, 41, 44–45, 47–48, 51, 55, 62, 68, 72–73, 78–79, 99, 107; capital, 6, 17, 21, 33, 88, 99; capitalist, xviii, 16, 44, 77; enslaved iv, viii–ix, xii–xviii, 1–11, 13, 15–19, 21–26, 31–59, 63, 65, 68–76, 78–81, 83–90, 92, 97–101, 111; global, xvii, xx, 5–6, 31–32, 39, 52–53, 107; pay, 2, 6, 11, 16, 18–21, 23, 28, 42, 57, 59–60, 63, 71, 74–75, 86, 91, 101; payment, xv–xvi, 7, 18–20, 23, 26–28, 39, 54, 75, 86, 90–91, 99, 101; planter, v, xi–xviii, xx, 1–4, 6–11, 15–27, 29, 31, 33–48, 51–53, 55–58, 62–63, 65–77, 79–80, 83–94, 97–102, 104; planter elite, xiii–xiv, 71; plantocracy, xiv, 16, 66, 69, 77, 89, 98, 100–101. *See also* land; wealth, ix, xvi–xvii, xx, 1–3, 6–7, 15–17, 24, 31, 34, 37, 45, 69, 72, 77, 90–91, 94, 97–98, 103, 105, 111
class, iv, xiii–xv, xix–xx, 1–3, 8–10, 12, 16, 34, 36, 56, 66, 70, 80, 83, 85, 87, 91, 93, 97–99, 102, 107, 110–111; managerial, iii–iv, xiv–xviii, 34–35, 44, 52, 91, 94, 102–3, 107; money, viii, 2, 16, 18, 20–21, 26, 28, 44–45, 60, 63, 67; poor, xiv, xx, 1–3, 9–10, 12, 15, 17, 24–26, 69, 78–80, 104, 107, 109; poor whites, xx, 2, 9–10, 12, 24, 26, 107–109; social, iv–v, ix, xiii–xvii, xx, 3, 9, 12, 37, 52, 56, 65–67, 69–73, 75, 77, 79, 81, 83, 85, 87–89, 91–95, 97, 102, 107–109, 113; society, xii–xvi, xviii–xx, 1, 3, 5, 8, 12, 16, 56, 61, 77, 87, 112; status, v, ix, xii, xv–xvi, 2–3, 8–9, 15, 19, 21, 36–37, 85–86, 93, 98, 110
Confederate (Civil War and Confederacy), 98–105, 109–111, 115; Confederacy, 98–99, 101, 103–5; Confederate States, 98, 101–5; Conscript, 100, 102; conscripted, 99; conscription, 98, 100, 102, 104–5; exempt, 99–101, 104; militia, 100
contested, 72
contract (law and relationships), iii–v, xiii–xviii, 1, 3–9, 11–13, 18, 20–24, 26–29, 34, 36–38, 41–44, 52, 55, 57–58, 62, 68–69, 71, 73, 76, 78, 80, 83, 87–91, 93–95, 99–100, 108, 110–112; contractual, v, xvi, 1, 3, 5–9, 11, 13,

20, 27, 36, 43, 67–68, 76, 87–88, 91, 102; employment, iv, xi, xiii–xvi, xviii, 1–2, 4, 7, 20–21, 26–27, 36–37, 42–44, 58, 60, 69–70, 73, 76, 83, 87, 89, 99–100, 102–3; employment contract, iv, xiv, xvi, 4, 7, 26, 36, 42, 58, 69, 73, 76, 83, 89, 99–100; employment relationship, xiii–xv, xvii; entitlements, 8–9; food (contracts for), 18–20, 26, 35–36, 43, 74, 88; modern, iv, xiii, 4–5, 7, 11, 13, 34, 102–3, 112; moral, 2, 39, 46, 87–89, 93; morality (clauses in), xvi–xvii, 39, 87, 89, 93; overseer contract, iii–iv, xiii, xvi–xviii, 9, 20–22, 24, 27–29, 34, 37, 42, 55, 62, 68–69, 78, 93–95; property theory of, 4, 7, 13, 112; relations, xiii–xv, xx, 6, 36, 45, 55, 67–68, 72, 77, 92, 108–109; supplies, 16, 22, 45; title theory of, 4, 7

control (in overseer management), v, xiv–xvii, 9, 16, 21, 31, 34–35, 41, 43–44, 46, 52, 59, 65–75, 77, 79, 81, 84, 86–87, 92, 98, 102, 107–109; lawsuits concerning authority and control in overseer management: *Alfred v. State*, 78, 113; *Graham v. Roark*, 92, 113; *Harmon v. Fleming*, 55, 114; *Jacob v. Ursuline Nuns*, 54, 114; *James v. Clarke County*, 85, 92, 114; *Lindsay v. Griffin*, 84, 92, 114; *Molett v. State*, 61, 114; *Nelson v. Botts*, 78, 114; *Porter v. Thomas*, 86, 92, 114; *Prichard v. Martin*, 40, 58, 90, 94, 114; *Richardson v. Pumphrey*, 9, 55, 114; *State v. Abram*, 75, 81, 114

court, viii, xvi, xxi, 5, 9, 21–23, 26, 35–42, 54–60, 71–72, 74–76, 80–81, 84–86, 90, 99–103, 105, 112

crime, 42, 75

damage, xix, 1, 21–22, 37–40

economy, iii–iv, viii, xiii–xiv, xvi–xviii 1–7, 11, 16, 19, 25, 29, 32–34, 36, 39, 41, 52, 68, 71, 77, 97, 107, 109, 111–112; collateral, 1, 6, 12, 16; commercial, 5–6, 10, 54, 112; credit, xx, 6, 12, 16–20, 25–26, 45, 93; economic, iv, xii–xvii, xix, xxi, 1, 3, 5, 9, 16–17, 19–20, 22, 25–26, 43, 45, 52–54, 62, 66, 83, 90, 102, 109, 111–113; fungible (goods), 5, 7; global economy, xvii; global marketplace, 6; hypothecate (land and labor), 16; instrument (financial), 4–7, 12, 42; investment, xix, 7, 11, 16–17, 19, 21, 49, 72, 88, 91, 98, 109; loan, 6; market, xvi–xvii, 4–7, 12, 16, 26, 31, 39, 43, 48, 90, 111. *See also* capitalism; mortgage (on enslaved persons), xi–xii, 6, 12, 16; percentage, xiv, 17, 19–20, 22, 25, 27–28; plantation economy, iii–iv, viii, xiii–xiv, xvi–xviii, 1–7, 19, 29, 33–34, 36, 39, 41, 52, 68, 71, 77, 97; salary, 2, 9, 17–20, 22, 25–28, 43, 57–58, 71, 90–91; slave, xi–xii, xv, xvii–xviii, xx, 1–3, 6–7, 10–12, 16–17, 26, 29, 31, 33–36, 38–40, 42, 45, 47–48, 52–54, 56–57, 59–61, 63, 65–66, 70, 73, 75–77, 79, 90, 98–99, 102–4, 106–110, 112–114; slavery, xii, xvii, xx–xxi, 7, 9–12, 24, 32–35, 52–54, 56, 58, 62–63, 66, 75, 78, 97, 103–4, 107–112; transaction, 6, 25; wealth, ix, xvi–xvii, xx, 1–3, 6–7, 15–17, 24, 31, 34, 37, 45, 69, 72, 77, 90–91, 94, 97–98, 103, 105, 111

enslaved, iv, viii–ix, xii–xviii, 1–11, 13, 15–19, 21–26, 31–59, 63, 65, 68–76, 78–81, 83–90, 92, 97–101, 111; bite (self-defense), 75. *See also* punishment; care of, 3, 21, 36, 42–43, 52, 55, 73–76, 80, 83–84, 86, 92; chattel, xi, 6–7; commodity, xvii, 4–7, 19, 72, 76, 102; death (by overseer), v, viii, xi–xii, xvi 15, 23, 27, 32–33, 37–41, 45, 52, 54, 57–58, 72–73, 75–76, 79, 83, 85–87, 89, 91, 93, 95; difficult (temperament), 15,

37, 39, 42; enslaver, xi–xii, xiv–xv, xvii, xx, 25, 29, 35, 45, 80–81, 84, 99; fit (healthy), 32, 34, 75, 78; ill, 74; injure, 45; injury of, 21, 35, 39, 57–58, 75, 90; management of, iv–v, xiii–xvi, xviii, 2–4, 6–10, 22, 24, 29, 31, 33–34, 38–39, 42–46, 48, 52–54, 59, 62–63, 67, 72–74, 76, 79–80, 87, 90, 97, 99–100, 102–3, 107, 110–112; mortgage on, xi–xii, 6, 12, 16; murder, xii, 38, 41; mutilate, 39; own, xii, xv–xvi, xx, 2, 8, 16–19, 24, 26, 31–32, 41–42, 44, 52, 56, 59–61, 65–69, 78–79, 86, 88, 91, 99; ownership, xiii–xv, 3, 7–8, 16–17, 19, 21, 26, 29, 34, 43, 45, 52, 70–71, 86, 98; pregnant, 33, 39, 74; rest for, 6, 75; rough (temperament), 37; saucy (temperament), 37; sex with, 47, 50, 63, 72; sick, 33, 36, 47, 52, 70, 73–76, 79–80; sickness, 35, 42, 73–76, 80; slave, xi–xii, xv, xvii–xviii, xx, 1–3, 6–7, 10–12, 16–17, 26, 29, 31, 33–36, 38–40, 42–45, 47–48, 52–54, 56–57, 59–61, 63, 65–66, 70, 73, 75–77, 79, 90, 98–99, 102–4, 106–110, 112–114; slave driver, 10, 34, 110; slavery, xi, xvii, xx–xxi, 7, 9–12, 24, 32–35, 52–54, 56, 58, 62–63, 66, 75, 78, 97, 103–4, 107–112; sound (healthy), 26; ungovernable (temperament), 39, 57; use, xx, 6, 11, 21, 24, 27, 34, 40, 48, 54, 59–60, 68–73, 77–78, 85–86, 88–89. *See also* plantation; valuation, 9, 26, 45, 47–48, 51, 55, 63; value, xiii, xviii, 2, 5–7, 11, 17, 25–27, 34, 39, 43, 45–51, 57–58, 62–63, 78–79, 86; whip, xi, 32–34, 36–37, 41, 54, 58, 72–73, 75, 79, 103; whipping, 32, 36, 39, 46, 54, 73, 79; work, vii–ix, xiii, xvii–xix, xxi, 2–4, 6, 9, 19, 21–22, 26, 32, 34, 37, 42, 44, 46, 48, 51–54, 59, 63, 66–67, 69–72, 74–77, 85, 88, 90, 94–95, 97, 100, 103, 106; worked, xiv, 1, 10, 15–18, 21–23, 43–44, 48, 51–52, 54–56, 71, 79, 100–101; working, xix, 2, 10, 13, 24, 31–32, 34, 45, 48, 54, 71, 110
executor (will), 86, 100

gender, viii, xiii–xv, xix–xx, 1, 66, 68, 77, 109, 111–112; gendered, xiv–xv, 8, 66, 68; identity, iii–iv, xiii–xix, 24, 65, 76, 103, 108–109, 111; manhood, 3, 9, 41, 65, 68, 77–78, 109. *See also* masculinities
ginning, 52, 70

homosocial, 68

illness, 73–76, 80. *See* masculinities
incompetent, 74. *See* mismanagement
injury (to enslaved), 21, 35, 39, 57–58, 75, 90; lawsuits concerning injury and death of the enslaved: *Brunson v. Martin*, 56, 113; *Cox v. State*, 58, 113; *Dowling v. State*, 59, 113; *Dwyer v. Cane*, 40, 58, 113; *Gillian v. Senter*, 57, 113; *Hendricks v. Phillips*, 40, 58, 114; *Johnson v. Lovett*, 57, 114; *Jordan v. State*, 40, 114; *Kennedy v. Mason*, 57, 114; *Martineau v. Hooper*, 57, 114; *Miller v. Stewart*, 57, 114; *Prichard v. Martin*, 40, 58, 90, 94, 114; *State v. Flanigin*, 41, 114; *Taylor v. Paterson*, 58, 114; *Womack v. Nicholson*, 57, 114

labor, iv, viii, xii–xviii, 1–4, 6–13, 15–19, 21–27, 31–37, 42–48, 52–53, 55–56, 59, 63, 68–73, 75–76, 78–79, 83–86, 88, 90, 97–99, 102, 110, 112; enslaved, iv, viii–ix, xii–xviii, 1–11, 13, 15–19, 21–26, 31–59, 63, 65, 68–76, 78–81, 83–90, 92, 97–101, 111; free, vii, ix, xii, 8, 18, 54–55, 59–60, 65, 97, 100; gang system of labor, 31, 46, 53–54; gin, 31, 69–70; ginning, 52, 70; hoe, 11, 32, 34, 53, 70; labored, 1, 15; laborers, xvi–xx,

1–2, 6, 12, 15, 17–18, 24–25, 31, 42, 44, 46, 66, 72–74, 76, 79, 88, 97, 100–101, 107; manage, 2–3, 7, 9, 15, 22, 37, 42, 56, 83, 86, 99–101; managing, v, xvi, 21, 31, 33–35, 37, 39, 41, 43, 45, 47, 49, 51–53, 55, 57, 59, 61, 63, 76, 88, 102; picking (cotton), 32, 52, 54, 70; reproductive labor, 6, 70, 72; slave driver, 10, 34, 110; supplies (plantation), 16, 22, 45; task system of labor, 7, 48, 56, 71, 74, 83, 85, 90–91

land, iv, xii–xvii, 1–3, 6, 9, 11, 15–19, 21, 24–27, 34, 42–44, 52–55, 66, 68–69, 79, 83–85, 92, 94, 98, 105, 112; acre, 15, 17–18, 25, 31, 33, 66; acreage, 17; credit, xx, 6, 12, 16–20, 25–26, 45, 93. *See also* economy; farm, 16–17, 24–25, 27, 76–77, 84, 87, 93, 99, 101–2. *See also* plantation; own, xii, xv–xvi, xx, 2, 8, 16–19, 24, 26, 31–32, 41–42, 44 52, 56, 59–61, 65–69, 78–79, 86, 88, 91, 99; ownership, xiii–xv, 3, 7–8, 16–17, 19, 21, 26, 29, 34, 43, 45, 52, 70–71, 86, 98; plantation, iii–v, viii–ix, xi–xviii, xx, 1–10, 15–29, 31–64, 66–68, 70–74, 76–80, 83–88, 90–95, 97, 99–104, 106–107, 110–113; tax, xviii, 23, 47–49, 63; taxation, 45–46, 48, 63

law, iv–v, vii–viii, xii, xiv–xvi, xviii, xxi, 4–8, 10–13, 34–36, 38–43, 46, 54, 56, 58–61, 65, 67–69, 71, 73, 75–77, 79, 81, 83–84, 87, 97–98, 100–105, 107–110, 112, 114–115; appeal, 21, 57, 59, 80, 101; appealed, 21, 41, 55, 57–58, 71, 75, 84–85, 101; appellate, 21–22, 41, 71–72, 90; code (criminal), xvi, 35–36, 39, 41–48, 56–57, 59–61, 63, 66, 83, 85, 114; common law, xiii, xvi, xxi, 3–4, 8, 24, 39, 44–45, 48, 71, 73, 83–84, 87, 92, 109, 111; criminal law and proceedings, xviii, 36–38, 40–41, 44, 75; equitable, 4–5; equity, 4–5, 97–99; estate, 15, 26–27, 33, 39, 57, 63, 75, 84, 86, 106, 114; felony, 38; judge, 4, 10, 38, 40, 75; private law, iv–v, xiv–xvi, xviii–xix, 34, 36, 41, 56, 65, 67–69, 71, 73, 75, 77, 79, 81, 87, 105; probate, 75; prosecution (of overseers), 41, 61, 102; public law, iv, xiv–xvi, xviii–xix, 34, 39–41, 43, 60, 67–68, 73, 76, 85, 97–100, 104; regulate, 4, 87; regulation (of enslaved, overseers, and planters), v, xv–xvi, 12, 31, 38, 41–42, 98, 101; remedies, 4; sentence (criminal), 41; statutory law, 35–36, 48, 83–85, 100; testimony (by enslaved, overseers, and planters), 38, 40, 74; trespass, 38, 84; trial, 10, 21–22, 35–38, 40–41, 57–59, 61, 71–72, 74–76, 84–86, 90, 101–2; wages, xv–xvi, xix, 1, 7, 18–27, 29, 37–38, 43, 52, 55–58, 71, 76, 87–88, 90, 110; will, viii, 4–5, 7, 11, 21, 24, 26, 33–35, 42–43, 46, 67, 69, 72–73, 86, 88, 99, 102

management, iv–v, xiii–xvi, xviii, 2–4, 6–10, 22, 24, 29, 31, 33–34, 38–39, 42–46, 48, 52–54, 59, 62–63, 67, 72–74, 76, 79–80, 87, 90, 97, 99–100, 102–3, 107, 110–112; authority (scope), xvi–xvii, 15, 34–39, 41–43, 45–46, 52, 59, 61, 65–66, 69, 71–72, 75, 84–86, 90, 98, 103–4; class, iv, xiii–xv, xix–xx, 1–3, 8–10, 12, 16, 34, 36, 56, 66, 70, 80, 83, 85, 87, 91, 93, 97–99, 102, 107, 110–111. *See also* capitalism; competent (as determined by planters and courts), 21, 34, 44, 84, 90; control (scope), v, xiv–xvii, 9, 16, 21, 31, 34–35, 41, 43–44, 46, 52, 59, 65–75, 77, 79, 81, 84, 86–87, 92, 98, 102, 107–109; cotton (picking monitored by), vii, xvii, xx–xxi, 4–6, 10–12, 17–20, 22–28, 31–34, 37–40, 43–55, 62–64, 70, 79, 83, 90–92, 97–98, 103, 107–112; crop (managed by), xvi, xviii, 3, 16–19, 21–22, 26–27, 33, 37, 40, 45–46, 48, 71, 83–84,

Index

90–91, 95; duties, xv–xvii, 3, 18, 20, 32, 35–36, 40, 42–44, 62–63, 66–68, 70, 78–79, 85–87, 93, 95; duty, xii, xv–xvii, 3, 9, 18, 20, 32, 35–36, 39–40, 42–46, 59, 62–63, 66–68, 70, 72–73, 78–79, 84–87, 90, 93, 95; employ, 23, 26, 39, 43, 63, 84, 99; employee, xv, 20, 42, 68, 84–85, 88, 94, 102–3, 106; employer (planter), xvi, 16, 19–21, 34–36, 40, 44, 59–61, 67–68, 84–85, 87–88, 91, 94, 99, 102; employment (on plantations), iv, xi, xiii–xvi, xviii, 1–2, 4, 7, 20–21, 26–27, 36–37, 42–44, 58, 60, 69–70, 73, 76, 83, 87, 89, 99–100, 102–3; George Washington, 3, 44, 67; gin, 31, 69–70; ill, 74; journal, xvi–xviii, 9, 12, 52, 54, 112–113; managed, xiv, 15, 17–18, 31, 40–41, 79, 83, 86, 101–2; manager, xii, 3, 9–10, 31, 34–35, 44, 52, 55, 62–63, 68–69, 73, 76–77, 87, 89, 98, 102–3, 106, 111; managerial identity, iii–iv, xvi, xviii, 103; managing, v, xvi, 21, 31, 33–35, 37, 39, 41, 43, 45, 47, 49, 51–53, 55, 57, 59, 61, 63, 76, 88, 102; manual, xiii, xv, 17–18, 25, 42–43, 45–46, 48, 62–63, 70, 74, 87–88; mismanagement (accusations of), xv, xviii, 21, 37–38, 41, 73, 76, 79–80, 84, 86; occupation, vii, 3, 47, 66, 97, 102; plantation, iii–v, viii–ix, xi–xviii, xx, 1–10, 15–29, 31–64, 66–68, 70–74, 76–80, 83–88, 90–95, 97, 99–104, 106–107, 110–113; profession, 18, 23, 66, 68–69; record, iv, vii–viii, xvii, 9, 15, 26–28, 34, 40, 44–49, 51, 55, 62–64, 73, 79, 103, 107, 112–113; salary, 2, 9, 17–20, 22, 25–28, 43, 57–58, 71, 90–91; sick (management of sickness), 33, 36, 47, 52, 70, 73–76, 79–80; station (position in society), 1, 66, 68, 72; Thomas Affleck, 9, 43–44, 62–63, 67, 71, 73, 78–79, 88, 91, 93, 95, 112

masculinities, iii–v, xiii, xv–xvi, 65–69, 71–73, 75, 77, 79, 81, 83, 86, 103, 112; hegemonic, xiii, xix–xx, 9, 66, 68–69, 71, 73, 77, 79, 112; identity, iii–iv, xiii–xix, 24, 65, 76, 103, 108–109, 111; male, iv, xiii–xvii, 2, 9, 40, 66, 94, 97, 106; maleness, xiii–xv, 2, 8–9. *See also* masculinities; man, iv–v, viii, xi–xvii, xx, 1–2, 4–10, 13, 15, 17, 19, 24–26, 32–36, 38–43, 45–46, 52, 54–59, 63, 65–77, 79, 83, 85–87, 89–93, 95, 100–105, 109, 112; manhood, 3, 9, 41, 65, 68, 77–78; masculine, 52, 73, 76; masculinity, iii–v, xiii, xv–xvi, xviii–xx, 8–9, 65–73, 75–79, 81, 83, 85–86, 103, 111–112; social, iv–v, ix, xiii–xvii, xx, 3, 9, 12, 37, 52, 56, 65–67, 69–73, 75, 77, 79, 81, 83, 85, 87–89, 91–95, 97, 102, 107–109, 113; white, iii–v, xi–xx, 1–3, 6–10, 12–13, 15–17, 24–26, 29, 34–36, 41–43, 45, 52, 55–56, 59, 61–62, 65–73, 75, 77–81, 85–87, 97, 101–110. *See also* white supremacy

mismanagement, xv, xviii, 21, 37–38, 41, 73, 76, 79–80, 84, 86; lawsuits concerning overseer mismanagement: *Dupree v. Prescott*, 80; *Lynch v. McRee*, 80, 114; *Peake v. Scaife*, 80, 114; *Prichard v. Martin*, 40, 58, 90, 94, 114; *Thompson v. Bertrand*, 74, 80, 114

negligence, xvii, 84

opinion xiii, 3, 55, 65, 74, 76, 79, 88, 101–2

overseers, iii–v, viii, xi–xviii, 1–11, 13, 31–46, 48, 52–63, 65–81, 83–95, 97–104, 106–107, 110–112; authority, xvi–xvii, 15, 34–39, 41–43, 45–46, 52, 59, 61, 65–66, 69, 71–72, 75, 84–86, 90, 98, 103–4; control (scope), v, xiv–xvii, 9, 16, 21, 31, 34–35, 41, 43–44, 46, 52, 59, 65–75, 77, 79, 81, 84, 86–87, 92, 98, 102, 107–109. *See also* enslaved; drink (alcohol), xii, 43, 69; duty (scope), xii, xv–xvii, 3, 9, 18, 20, 32, 35–36, 39–40, 42–46, 59, 62–63, 66–68, 70, 72–73, 78–79, 84–87, 90, 93, 95; employ, 23, 26, 39, 43, 63, 84, 99; employee, xv, 20, 42, 68, 84–85, 88, 94, 102–3, 106. *See also* planter; employing, 33, 40, 53, 85; employment, iv, xi, xiii–xvi, xviii, 1–2, 4, 7, 20–21, 26–27, 36–37, 42–44, 58, 60, 69–70, 73, 76, 83, 87, 89, 99–100, 102–3; immoral, v, xvi, 40, 83, 85, 87, 89, 91, 93, 95; intoxication, 43; managerial identity, iii–iv, xvi, xviii, 103; men, iv–v, viii, xi–xvii, xx, 1–2, 4–10, 13, 15, 17, 24–25, 34–36, 40–43, 45–46, 52, 54–55, 63, 65–66, 68–69, 71–74, 83, 85–87, 89, 91–93, 95, 100–102, 105, 109. *See also* masculinities; mismanagement, xv, xviii, 21, 37–38, 41, 73, 76, 79–80, 84, 86; moral, 2, 39, 46, 87–89, 93; morality, xvi–xvii, 39, 87, 89, 93; occupation, vii, 3, 47, 66, 97, 102; overseership, 3, 10, 23, 26; profession, 18, 23, 66, 68–69; responsibility, xv, 1, 7, 9, 36, 39, 43–44, 74, 83–84, 88, 91; salaries, 2, 17–20, 25–28, 91; spirits (alcohol), 37, 43, 69, 88; station (position in society), 1, 66, 68, 72; work, vii–ix, xiii, xvii–xix, xxi, 2–4, 6, 9, 19, 21–22, 26, 32, 34, 37, 42, 44, 46, 48, 51–54, 59, 63, 66–67, 69–72, 74–77, 85, 88, 90, 94–95, 97, 100, 103, 106

patriarchy, xii, 34, 66; authority, xvi–xvii, 15, 34–39, 41–43, 45–46, 52, 59, 61, 65–66, 69, 71–72, 75, 84–86, 90, 98, 103–4. *See also* masculinities; father, vii, 10, 23, 36, 39, 41, 54, 56, 65–66, 72, 85, 87, 94, 103; identity, iii–iv, xiii–xix, 24, 65, 76, 103, 108–109, 111; obligation, xv–xvi, xviii, 36, 42–44, 55–56, 67, 76, 80, 83, 87, 102; paternal, 37, 39, 85; patriarch, 65, 73, 77; patriarchal, 9, 15, 29, 44, 52, 66, 72; planter paternalism, 10

plantation, iii–v, viii–ix, xi–xviii, xx, 1–10, 15–29, 31–64, 66–68, 70–74, 76–80, 83–88, 90–95, 97, 99–104, 106–107, 110–113; Alabama, xvii–xviii, 15, 17–18, 24–26, 35–36, 38–39, 41–42, 46–49, 56–57, 59–61, 63, 75, 84–85, 98, 100–102, 106, 114; antebellum, ix–xii, xiv, xvi, 1–3, 6, 8–10, 16, 24–26, 31, 34, 56, 65–66, 70, 72–73, 85, 97, 107–112; Arkansas, xvii–xviii, 19, 37–38, 46, 61, 63, 74, 84, 112, 114; cotton, vii, xvii, xx–xxi, 4–6, 10–12, 17–20, 22–28, 31–34, 37–40, 43–55, 62–64, 70, 79, 83, 90–92, 97–98, 103, 107–112; credit, xx, 6, 12, 16–20, 25–26, 45, 93. *See also* economy; crop, xvi, xviii, 3, 16–19, 21–22, 26–27, 33, 37, 40, 43, 45–46, 48, 71, 83–84, 90–91, 95; food (supplied to), 18–20, 26, 35–36, 43, 74, 88; Georgia, xvii–xviii, 15, 17–18, 23–24, 35–36, 39, 41, 46, 48, 56, 63, 83, 86, 89, 94, 98, 103–4, 108–112, 114; hoe, 11, 32, 34, 53, 70; implements (farming), 16–17, 67; labor, iv, viii, xii–xviii, 1–4, 6–13, 15–19, 21–27, 31–37, 42–48, 52–53, 55–56, 59, 63, 66, 68–73, 75–76, 78–79, 83–86, 88, 90, 97–99, 102, 110, 112; land, iv, xii–xvii, 1–3, 6, 9, 11, 15–19, 21, 24–27, 34, 42–44, 52–55, 66, 68–69, 79, 83–85, 92, 94, 98, 105, 112; Louisiana, xi, xvii–xviii, xx–xxi, 9, 12, 17, 21–22, 24–25, 39–40, 54, 57–58, 63, 79, 104, 108–112; master, xii, xiv, xx, 3, 5, 8, 10–11, 24, 33, 35–36, 38–39, 53, 56–57, 59–63, 75, 79, 84, 95, 107, 109–113; Mississippi, xvii–xviii, xx, 17, 24–25, 35–36, 40–41, 46, 48, 56, 59–61, 72, 80, 83, 90, 98, 104, 107, 115; overseer, iii–v, viii, xi–xviii, 1–11, 13, 15–29, 31–46,

48, 52–63, 65–81, 83–95, 97–104, 106–107, 110–112; planter, v, xi–xviii, xx, 1–4, 6–11, 15–27, 29, 31, 33–48, 51–53, 55–58, 62–63, 65–77, 79–80, 83–94, 97–102, 104. *See also* masculinities; plantocracy, xiv, 16, 66, 69, 77, 89, 98, 100–101; slave driver, 10, 34, 110; south, iv, vii–viii, xii, xiv–xvi, xix, xxi, 1–2, 5–6, 8–10, 12, 16–18, 23–26, 29, 31, 34, 46, 55–56, 62, 65–66, 72, 77, 79–80, 92–94, 97, 107–112; southern, iv, vii, xiii, xv–xx, 1–3, 10–12, 16, 23–25, 41, 48, 53, 55–56, 58, 65–66, 73, 77, 83, 92–93, 95, 98, 103, 107–113; tax, xviii, 23, 47–49, 63; taxation, 45–46, 48, 63; work, vii–ix, xiii, xvii–xix, xxi, 2–4, 6, 9, 19, 21–22, 26, 32, 34, 37, 42, 44, 46, 48, 51–54, 59, 63, 66–67, 69–72, 74–77, 85, 88, 90, 94–95, 97, 100, 103, 106

planter, v, xi–xviii, xx, 1–4, 6–11, 15–27, 29, 31, 33–48, 51–53, 55–58, 62–63, 65–77, 79–80, 83–94, 97–102, 104; authority, xvi–xvii, 15, 34–39, 41–43, 45–46, 52, 59, 61, 65–66, 69, 71–72, 75, 84–86, 90, 98, 103–4; control, v, xiv–xvii, 9, 16, 21, 31, 34–35, 41, 43–44, 46, 52, 59, 65–75, 77, 79, 81, 84, 86–87, 92, 98, 102, 107–109; credit, xx, 6, 12, 16–20, 25–26, 45, 93. *See also* economy; duties, xv–xvii, 3, 18, 20, 32, 35–36, 40, 42–44, 62–63, 66–68, 70, 78–79, 85–87, 93, 95; duty, xii, xv–xvii, 3, 9, 18, 20, 32, 35–36, 39–40, 42–46, 59, 62–63, 66–68, 70, 72–73, 78–79, 84–87, 90, 93, 95; elite, xiii–xvi, xx, 66, 71, 80; employ, 23, 26, 39, 43, 63, 84, 99; employer, xvi, 16, 19–21, 34–36, 40, 44, 59–61, 67–68, 84–85, 87–88, 91, 94, 99, 102; employment, iv, xi, xiii–xvi, xviii, 1–2, 4, 7, 20–21, 26–27, 36–37, 42–44, 58, 60, 69–70, 73, 76, 83, 87, 89, 99–100, 102–3; enslaver, xi–xii, xiv–xv, xvii, xx, 25, 29, 35, 45, 80–81, 84, 99; father, vii, 10, 23, 36, 39, 41, 54, 56, 65–66, 72, 85, 87, 94, 103. *See also* patriarch; identity, iii–iv, xiii–xix, 24, 65, 76, 103. *See also* gender; man, iv–v, viii, xi–xii, xx, 1–2, 4–10, 13, 15, 17, 19, 24–26, 32–36, 38–43, 45–46, 52, 54–59, 63, 65–77, 79, 83, 85–87, 89–93, 95, 100–105, 109, 112; master, xii, xiv, xx, 3, 5, 8, 10–11, 24, 33, 35–36, 38–39, 53, 56–57, 59–63, 75, 79, 84, 95, 107, 109–113. *See also* masculinities; men, iv–v, viii, xi–xvii, xx, 1–2, 4–10, 13, 15, 17, 24–25, 34–36, 40–43, 45–46, 52, 54–56, 63, 65–66, 68–69, 71–74, 83, 85–87, 89, 91–93, 95, 100–102, 105, 109; money, viii, 2, 16, 18, 20–21, 26, 28, 44–45, 60, 63, 67; obligation, xv–xvi, xviii, 36, 42–44, 55–56, 67, 76, 80, 83, 87, 102; owner, iv, xi–xii, 6–7, 9, 19, 29, 34–36, 39–40, 42, 45, 52, 55–57, 59–61, 63, 68, 75, 84, 86–87, 102–3, 109; paternal, 37, 39, 85; planter elite, xii–xiv, 71. *See also* class; planter paternalism, 10; plantocracy, xiv, 16, 66, 69, 77, 89, 98, 100–101; slaveholder, xx, 2, 8, 36, 97, 110

punishment (and torture of the enslaved), 32, 34–36, 38–40, 46, 53–54, 73, 103; beating, 39–41, 58; blood, 32, 40; convict (convictions concerning), 41; court, vii, xvi, xxi, 5, 9, 21–23, 26, 35–42, 54–60, 71–72, 74–76, 80–81, 84–86, 90, 99–103, 105, 112; criminal, xvii, 36–38, 40–41, 44, 75; cruel, 3, 33, 35–36, 40, 69; cruelty, 33–34, 36, 40, 56–57; death, v, viii, xi–xii, xvi, 15, 23, 27, 32–33, 37–41, 45, 52, 54, 57–58, 72–73, 75–76, 79, 83, 85–87, 89, 91, 93, 95; discipline, 34, 39, 44, 72; hang, xi–xii, 54; hanging, xi–xii, xix; judge, 4, 10, 38, 40, 75; kill, 37, 84; lynch, 80, 114; lynching, 6; maim, 39; murder, xii, 38, 41, 72; punish, 38, 55; punishing, xviii, 38, 73; punishment, 32, 34–36, 38–40, 46, 53–54, 73, 103; scarred, 74; shoot, 37; shooting, 37, 39, 58; slave, xi–xii, xv, xvii–xviii, xx, 1–3, 6–7, 10–12, 16–17, 26, 29, 31, 33–36, 38–40, 42–45, 47–48, 52–54, 56–57, 59–61, 63, 65–66, 70, 73, 75–77, 79, 90, 98–99, 102–4, 106–110, 112–114; slavery, xii, xvii, xx–xxi, 7, 9–12, 24, 32–35, 52–54, 56, 58, 62–63, 66, 75, 78, 97, 103–4, 107–112; stripes, 41, 57, 61; surveil, 31, 41; surveillance, xviii, 41, 43, 103; swollen, 74; torture, v, xvi, 31, 33, 35, 37, 39–41, 43, 45, 47, 49, 51, 53, 55, 57, 59, 61, 63; violence, v, xvi, 31, 33–37, 39, 41, 43, 45, 47, 49, 51, 53, 55, 57, 59, 61, 63, 72, 103, 110–111; wages, xv–xvi, xix, 1, 7, 18–27, 29, 37–38, 43, 52, 55–58, 71, 76, 87–88, 90, 110; whip, xi, 32–34, 36–37, 41, 54, 58, 72–73, 75, 79, 103; whipping, 32, 36, 39, 46, 54, 73, 79

pushing (rate of labor), v, viii, xvi, 31–33, 35, 37, 39, 41, 43, 45–47, 49, 51, 53–55, 57, 59, 61, 63

race, i, iii–iv, xii–xvi, xix–xx, 1, 9, 24, 66, 92, 97, 107–111; black, iv, vi–viii, xii, xvii, xix, 1, 10, 20, 24, 28–29, 54, 65, 103, 106; identity, iii–iv, xiii–xix, 24, 65, 76, 103, 108–109, 111; racial identity, xix, 108–109; whiteness, xiii–xv, xix, 2, 8–10, 68, 109–110, 112

record (plantation records), iv, vii–viii, xvii, 9, 15, 26–28, 34, 40, 44–49, 51, 55, 62–64, 73, 79, 103, 107, 112–113

Sabbath, 46, 63
salary, 2, 9, 17–20, 22, 25–28, 43, 57–58, 71, 90–91
sickness, 35, 42, 73–76, 80
sober, 87, 93
sobriety, 87, 89, 93–94

theory, xix, 4, 6–8, 13, 84, 109, 111–112

unequal, i, iii–iv, xiv, 102
unsound, 47, 74, 79, 99

wage, xv–xvi, xix, 1–4, 7, 12, 15, 18–27, 29, 37–38, 43, 52, 55–58, 71, 76, 87–88, 90, 97, 110; lawsuits concerning non-payment of wages: *Cresap v. Winter*, 21, 23, 29, 113; *Garcia v. Garcia*, 22, 29, 113; *Lambert v. King*, 22, 29, 113; *Pettigrew v. Bishop*, 29, 114; *Roberts v. Brownrigg*, 29, 114; *Whitley v. Murray*, 62, 114

War (Civil), 27, 49, 97–99, 101–2, 104, 108–110, 113; lawsuits concerning overseer conscription & exemption during the Civil War: *Ex parte Graham*, 104–5, 113; *In re Strawbridge*, 105, 114

watch, 70, 106. *See* enslaved
white supremacy, iv, xiii, xix, 34, 66, 97; identity, iii–iv, xiii–xix, 24, 65, 76, 103, 108–109, 111; managerial identity, iii–iv, xvi, xviii, 103. *See also* masculinities; paternal, 37, 39, 85; paternalism, 10, 36, 52, 56, 108; patriarchal, 9, 15, 29, 44, 52, 66, 72; white, iii–v, xi–xx, 1–3, 6–10, 12–13, 15–17, 24–26, 29, 34–36, 41–43, 45, 52, 55–56, 59, 61–62, 65–73, 75, 77–81, 85–87, 97, 101–110; whiteness, xiii–xv, xix, 2, 8–10, 68, 109–110, 112

yeoman, xi–xii, xiv–xv, xx, 2–3, 6–7, 16–17, 24–25, 66, 109; dependent, xiv–xv, 3, 5, 10, 16, 37, 66, 68, 72, 77; farmer, xi, 1, 3, 7, 10, 16–17, 24–26, 66, 87, 99, 101, 104, 109; independence, xiv–xv, 3, 16, 18, 25, 52, 65; independent, xv, 3, 18, 26, 65, 68, 77

About the Author

Teri A. McMurtry-Chubb is a Professor of Law at UIC John Marshall Law School. She researches, teaches, and writes in the areas of critical rhetoric, discourse and genre analysis, and legal history. She is the author of numerous publications, including *In Search of the Common Law Inside the Black Female Body*, 114 Nw. U. L. Rev. Online 187 (2019) and *There Are No Outsiders Here: Rethinking Intersectionality as Hegemonic Discourse in the Age of #MeToo*, 16 Legal Comm. & Rhetoric: JALWD 1 (2019). Teri is a contributor to *Feminist Judgments: Rewritten Opinions of the United States Supreme Court* (2016), where she authored a rewritten opinion for the case *Loving v. Virginia* (1967). For her publication *The Rhetoric of Race, Redemption, and Will Contests: Inheritance as Reparations in John Grisham's Sycamore Row*, 48 Univ. Memphis L. Rev. 890 (2018), she won 2018 Teresa Godwin Phelps Award for Scholarship in Legal Communication. Moreover, she is the recipient of the 2021 Thomas F. Blackwell Memorial Award for Outstanding Achievement in the Field of Legal Writing.

www.ingramcontent.com/pod-product-compliance
Lightning Source LLC
Chambersburg PA
CBHW020126010526
44115CB00008B/995